THE HAPPY CAMPER'S COOKBOOK

THE HAPPY CAMPER'S COOKBOOK
Eating Well Is Portable™

Marilyn Abraham
Sandy MacGregor

A Recreational Press Book
CLEAR LIGHT PUBLISHERS

*This book is dedicated to our parents
who first taught us about
good food and good eating.*

A Recreational Press Book
Published by
Clear Light Publishers, 823 Don Diego, Santa Fe, N.M. 87501

First Edition
10 9 8 7 6 5 4 3 2 1

Library of Congress Cataloging-in-Publication Data
Abraham, Marilyn, 1950-
    The Happy Camper's Cookbook / Marilyn Abraham
and Sandy MacGregor.
        p.   cm.
    ISBN   1-57416-024-9
    1. Outdoor cookery.   I. MacGregor, Sandy, 1942-
    II. Title.
    TX823.A27   1999
    641.5'78--dc21   98-49288
                                                                CIP

Cover photograph © Marcia Keegan
Interior photographs © Marilyn Abraham and Sandy MacGregor
Production and typography by Carol O'Shea

Printed in Canada

⬛ CONTENTS

2. SEVERAL SOUPS, HOT & COLD 37

3. MAINS FROM THE GRILL & SMOKER... 45

4. INDOOR MAINS 65

🛣 (INTRO) EATING WELL IS PORTABLE

Welcome!
Camping and cooking.
Hamburgers and hot dogs.
Right?
Wrong.

While there's nothing wrong with a great burger or a done-up dog, cooking in the great outdoors has become a lot more than just those two old standbys. With the advent of portable grills, smokers and cook-tops, virtually anything is possible.

Why, then a special cookbook? This book assumes you have limited space, time, tools, and ingredients. We also assume that you've done some cooking in your life and we encourage you to use that experience, coupled with your family's preferences, to make these recipes your own.

A word about ingredients—two words, actually—PLEASE SUBSTITUTE. If you don't have mayonnaise, use yogurt or sour cream. If you prefer margarine to butter, feel free. If salt isn't in your diet, do what you must to season a dish. If you don't have tomato sauce, use tomato paste and water, or mix some reconstituted sun-dried tomatoes with fresh ones or canned. If you don't have that, see what you can do with ketchup. Just don't give up or get frustrated. There's something you can use—it's just hiding somewhere. Go ahead, use lemons instead of limes or vinegar. Substitute maple syrup for sugar or honey. Forget about the cinnamon if you don't have any and feel free to trade the thyme for oregano.

The abundance of simple yet delicious "new" ways to prepare food while traveling mirrors eating habits everywhere: salsa sales surpassed ketchup years ago; Asian influences, such as soy sauce and sesame oil, are in everyone's pantry; and bagels are as common as toast for breakfast. The ready availability of "new" ingredients challenges and allows us to have more variety in our meals, no matter where we happen to take them.

TOWNSEND, MONTANA

BREAKFAST ALERT!!! This town is right out of the 50's, and some of the prices are too. Of course we homed right in on the local bakery/restaurant where we had 2 eggs, 2 pieces of bacon, 2 pancakes for 2 bucks. Yum!

Our goal in this book is to share our enjoyment of and enthusiasm for good food through a variety of recipes and ideas. One of those ideas is that dinner is the meal that requires the most effort. We like tasty dinners at the end of our busy outdoor days. Dinners are long on satisfaction, but still short on preparation. The flip side of that idea is that we assume your breakfasts and lunches are, like our own, so simple they don't require recipes: no hot lunches, no buffet breakfasts, no noontime blue-plate specials. We'll pass on a few useful ideas as we go along about which left-overs make good lunches, for instance, but we basically assume you don't need any other advice from us on that front. Have some cereal, make a nice sandwich, check back with us at supper time.

Telluride,
Colorado

A word about altitude: When you're above 5,000 feet, you may experience technical difficulties. As air pressure decreases, so does the temperature at which water boils. It will take longer to make things such as pasta, rice, and beans. In baking, you'll experience a faster rise (again because of less pressure), but watch out for the thud when yeast breads collapse. Go easy on the rise components, that is, yeast and the sugars that feed them.

We've logged tens of thousands of miles throughout North America. As part of our enjoyment of traveling we've ferreted out hundreds of hidden bakeries in order to find a great donut or crusty loaf of bread and gone down many a dirt road to find a farm stand with the perfect peach, tomato, or cherry. From time to time serendipity has brought us to a gem of a barbecue joint or a five-star restaurant in the woods. But the truth is there's something magical about fashioning a meal to your taste, alone or with friends and family, as the sun goes down and the temperature begins to chill.

Whether you're cooking on an open fire or in a microwave, we believe that cooking while camping can be an experience in itself, an ode to all the senses at once. Imagine yourself in the place of your dreams. The sound of a waterfall, perhaps, in the background. The air feels just right and the vista is incredible. You're happy, relaxed, and hungry after a good walk. You think you smell something delicious. Could be the dinner of your dreams. So happy camping and, as they say, Bon Appetit!

KITCHEN UTENSILS

Basically, we think you really need very few. As often as possible, think double duty. The wok, for instance, can be used to fry, boil, steam, and stir fry. Mixing bowls are also salad bowls, and so on. Some essentials are listed below.

 TIP: SHARPEN UP! A sharp knife is safer to use than a dull one since it does its job smoothly and easily. Please carry a small sharpener. It will make you a better chef.

Utensil Essentials

Wok with lid
Pot large enough to make pasta
Large frying pan, preferably cast iron
2 mixing/microwavable/serving bowls, large and medium size
Baking dish (Pyrex, about 7″x 11″ or 8″x 8″)
Salad servers
Cutting board
Small and medium sharp knives
Long serrated knife
Wooden spoon
Ladle
Spatulas, one for scraping, and one for flipping
Strainer/colander
Vegetable peeler
Hot mitts
Grilling and smoking equipment (see pp. 11-14)

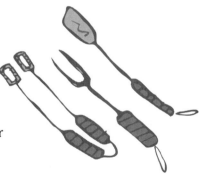

ABOUT THE PORTABLE PANTRY

Consider this your personal kitchen packing list. Add and delete according to your family's usage. Try not to make the mistake we did of packing months' worth of supplies. We can assure you there are grocery stores everywhere, plus specialty markets, farm stands, and regional goodies you'll want to pick up along the way.

 TIP: PANTRY TO GO. Transfer any dry items, such as herbs, flour, and sugar that are packaged in large containers into baggies, clean film canisters, or plastic containers. Wet ingredients can be transferred into plastic squeeze bottles for safe transport, slim storage, and easy use.

Wet Condiments

Olive oil
Cooking oil (corn, canola, peanut or other bland vegetable oil)
Balsamic vinegar
White vinegar
Ketchup
Mayonnaise
Soy sauce
Maple syrup and/or honey
Mustard
Hot sauce

TIP: EASY RIDER. Store large, heavy bowls upside down. They will ride more safely and quietly.

Dry Seasonings

Salt (we always use kosher salt)
Black pepper
Cayenne or red pepper flakes
Cumin powder
Curry
Chili powder
Cinnamon
Oregano
Rosemary
Sage
Thyme

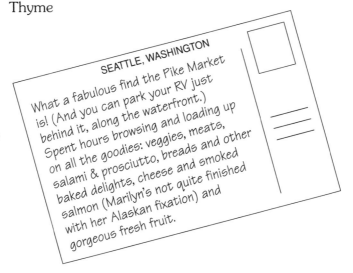

SEATTLE, WASHINGTON

What a fabulous find the Pike Market is! (And you can park your RV just behind it, along the waterfront.) Spent hours browsing and loading up on all the goodies: veggies, meats, salami & prosciutto, breads and other baked delights, cheese and smoked salmon (Marilyn's not quite finished with her Alaskan fixation) and gorgeous fresh fruit.

Pantry Basics

Pasta
Rice
Flour
Sugar (white/brown)
Baking powder, baking soda
Condensed, sweetened condensed, or powdered milk
Chocolate chips
Nuts and seeds
Raisins, prunes, apricots, and other dried fruits
Tomato sauce/paste
Couscous
Chick peas, pintos, other
  canned/dried beans
Broth or bouillon cubes
Peanut butter
Jam/jelly
Crackers
Cookies
Coffee/tea
Soda/water

 TIP: LIVE LARGE, THINK SMALL. Warehouse clubs have great prices, but huge quantities. Why not shop and share with friends? Then you can wrap, bag, and freeze.

Refrigerator Basics

Butter
Eggs
Milk
Parmesan cheese
Bread
Carrots
Garlic
Ginger
Onions
Potatoes
Lemons/limes

 TIP: ZIP IT. We use freezer thickness zip-lock bags to store as much as possible because they save space. Our friend, Alice R., taught us to suck the extra air out as well, making sure the bags take up even less space! When filling bags, try propping them up in a large bowl for support—it's like having an extra pair of hands. ANOTHER ZIP TIP: When reheating or thawing, vent your bag and microwave on the appropriate setting. Remove bag using hot mitts, and open carefully to avoid steam burns and spills.

Freezer Basics

One thing we always prefer fresh is hamburger. We think burgers taste best when the meat is bought and cooked the same day. If you have leftover meat after the burgers are done, however, you can freeze it for later use in meat sauce. Many things, if properly wrapped, do freeze well. Examples are listed below.

Steak, chicken, sausage, pork
Shrimp and salmon
Juices
Bagels/rolls/bread
Butter

 TIP: WHAT'S THAT THING? Wrap items first in plastic wrap, then in freezer bags in portions appropriate for your family. Either write the description and the date on the bag or place a slip of paper with the information in the bag.

Under the Sink

Baggies (zip-lock heavyweight, small and large)
Aluminum foil
Plastic wrap
Paper towels
Cleanser
Dish cloths
Scrub sponges
Dish washing soap
Extra plastic storage containers

OUTDOOR COOKING EQUIPMENT

Cooking outside is an integral part of camping. Once you get hooked on the taste of grilled food, you may find yourself hauling a smoker and several grills along on your travels. While we recommend specific types of equipment, if you're caught in a pinch, most of the recipes in this book can be prepared on whatever is available, such as a cement and iron BBQ pit or with a stick over an open fire. All that is required is a little ingenuity and courage.

Gas Grills

We prefer to bring along a portable gas BBQ when we camp. There are several important things to look for when you shop for a gas grill.

1. Check out the temperature range and controllability of the heat. Look for a grill with at least 12,000 BTU heat output (the more heat the better) and an easily adjusted gas valve.
2. The grill you use should have a cover or bonnet that can be closed while cooking.
3. The grill apparatus should be compact for easy handling and storage while providing the largest cooking surface possible.

We chose our portable grill because it heats to a higher temperature than many other brands and has a convenient built-in temperature gauge.

The gas for these grills is provided by small, disposable propane canisters which are available in all hardware and outdoor equipment stores. The canisters will run for about 3 to 4 hours. Some people have adapted larger propane tanks for use with portable grills, or use a connection to their motor home tank, which is available through catalogs.

Wood or Charcoal Grills

Some people prefer to cook over charcoal or wood. Certainly these grills will also work, and if you prefer this method here is what to look for. Keep in mind carrying and storage, and don't forget you have to stow the charcoal too.

1. Find a model that has a bonnet or cover for use while cooking.
2. Both the cover and the grill base should have easily adjustable air vents to regulate cooking temperature by adjusting air flow.
3. Again, the grill you use should provide easy handling and have the largest cooking surface possible.

Grills: Using What's Available

Many campsites come equipped with fire pits or concrete grills for use by picnickers and campers. We normally don't use this equipment because the grilling surface is frequently made of heavy iron which takes forever to heat and the surface of the grate can be filthy and/or very rusty. If you do use this type of equipment, get a very hot fire going at least 1 hour before you begin to cook in order to heat the heavy iron grate as well as sterilize it.

Smokers

Wood smoke adds a desirable flavor to many dishes. The best way to achieve this flavor is by using a very slow cooking smoker. The rule of smoking is low and slow. Slow cooking (220 degrees and under) also allows for the lengthy cooking times that tougher, less expensive cuts of meat require to become chewable. If you have unlimited space, or you're planning a fishing trip and know you'll be smoking your limit daily, you may wish to carry a dedicated smoker along. A slow cooking smoker allows you to infuse the taste of the wood of your choice (hickory, mesquite, etc.) into your food. In many smokers this infusion is accomplished by placing water-soaked wood chips or chunks over hot coals to provide dense, continuous smoke along with slow heat. The equipment you choose will not have high temperature capability and can be electrically heated, gas fired, or wood/charcoal burning. Smokers come in many varieties and are sold in well-equipped outdoor cooking sections of hardware and garden stores.

There is a simpler way to get that smoky flavor. We carry a small metal smoking box filled with wood which is used along with the gas grill. The wood chips are soaked in a bucket (or bowl or pot) of water for at least one hour, then put in the handy box and onto the grill surface of the covered BBQ. While this technique doesn't cook at as low a temperature as a smoker, and therefore, can't be used for smoke-tenderizing tough, inexpensive cuts of meat, it does provide the flavor we crave. And it is much easier than carrying around another piece of major equipment. Smoking boxes or wood chip containers are generally available at hardware and outdoor equipment stores.

On wood chips: If you plan on smoking food you'll need to carry wood or wood chips. We usually carry a bag of hickory chips, but mesquite chips are also readily available. Both can be found in the outdoor section of hardware stores or garden centers.

Grill Tools

Long-handled tool sets are generally available at hardware and kitchen stores. You should have a pair of clamps (tongs), a fork, and a spatula. It's also a good idea to have hot pads or a heat mitt to avoid getting burned. You can also find fire- and heat-resistant gloves made of asbestos. These come in especially handy when adding coal or wood to a fire, and removing hot coals from your grill after your meal.

Skewers

We use stainless steel skewers for making kabobs or grilling anything small that might otherwise fall through the grate of the grill. Some people prefer water-soaked wood skewers.

Instant-Read Meat Thermometer

A small, instant-read meat thermometer helps you cook to the desired doneness by measuring the internal temperature. These thermometers come with a plastic case, or sleeve, and the whole device slips into your shirt pocket like a pen. If you don't want to risk ruining a great steak (or whatever), use an instant-read thermometer to tell you when it is done. (For more detail, see the doneness table on pg. 47.)

RUBS, MARINADES, SAUCES, SALSAS & CHUTNEYS

This is what separates the wienies from the dogs at dinnertime around the old campfire. While we'll admit that certain things—burgers, for instance—can be perfect plain, other foods take on a lot more interest with just a little bit of enhancement from the chef either before cooking or at the table.

Later in the book you'll find recipes that use these rubs and marinades in specific combination with meat, poultry, fish and so forth. Please don't regard these as rules! Mix and match them in whatever way you like. Country Pork Rub, for instance, is not illegal on chicken, fish, or beef. Experiment with adding your favorite flavors to any of these recipes.

RUBS

Rubs are dry or pretty dry. And, surprise, you rub them onto the food. Rubs can be prepared ahead in quantity. Store them in a dark, cool place, in something airtight. Rub the food 2 to 24 hours before cooking, and then cover and refrigerate. Let the food stand at room temperature about 1 hour prior to cooking. This makes cooking quicker and the end result moister.

MARINADES

Marinades are liquids used to soak food before cooking. Marinades flavor and tenderize the food, usually through an acidic component. The longer the item to be cooked is left to soak, the more flavor it will pick up, but the rule of thumb is not less than 1 hour and not more than 24. Keep covered in the refrigerator until the last hour. Try marinating in zip lock bags for zero tolerance cleanup. To avoid bacterial contamination never reuse marinades. If you want to serve some at the table, set some aside at the beginning and use the remainder for soaking.

SAUCES, SALSAS, AND CHUTNEYS

These are meant to be passed along with the food at the table. You can make an extra batch of marinade, or mix your favorite rub with mayo or yogurt for a quick dip. Or try one of ours! Don't hesitate to try your own concoction.

If these recipes sound "intense," that's the point. Whatever you rub on the outside has to have a real punch to work itself all the way through the meat. Once the food is cooked, these rubs and marinades impart a rich flavor we relish.

Rubs

INSTANT STEAK RUB

Yield: About 1/4 cup
(4 tablespoons)

Here's the fastest, easiest way we know to dress up any beef steak.

3 tablespoons garlic/chili paste*
1 tablespoon brown sugar

* *You can find this product in the Asian section of your market.*

HAPPY PORK RUB

Yield: About 1/2 cup

We like this rub on pork roasts and pork chops cooked on our BBQ grill.

6 to 8 cloves garlic, minced
1 teaspoon salt
1/4 cup packed brown sugar
1 tablespoon balsamic vinegar
1 to 2 tablespoons chili powder
2 teaspoons ground cumin

Mash garlic and salt before combining with other ingredients.

On the Alaska Hwy

COUNTRY PORK RUB

Yield: About 1/2 cup

Here is a versatile rub we use on any meat we cook in our smoker.

6 cloves garlic, finely minced
1/2 teaspoon salt
1/4 cup packed brown sugar
1 to 2 tablespoons chili powder
1 teaspoon black pepper

Mash garlic and salt before combining with other ingredients.

C-RUB

Yield: About 1/4 cup

This is a variation of a recipe we discovered on a sailing trip with Captain Gwen out of St. Thomas. C-Rub and its brother C-Rub Plus are great on any cut of lamb that you are barbecuing.

1 tablespoon ground cumin
1 tablespoon curry powder
1 tablespoon coriander leaves, dried
1/4 teaspoon cayenne powder
1/2 teaspoon ground cinnamon

C-RUB PLUS

Yield: About 1/3 cup

Make this spreadable rub for coating larger pieces of meat or for soaking cubed meat for kabobs.

2 cloves garlic, finely minced
1/2 teaspoon salt
1 teaspoon ground cumin
1 teaspoon curry powder
1/2 teaspoon black pepper
1/4 teaspoon cayenne powder
1/4 teaspoon ground cinnamon
1/4 cup plain yogurt OR
    juice of 1/2 lemon and 2 tablespoons olive oil

Mash garlic and salt before combining with other ingredients.

FAJITA RUB

Yield: 2 to 3 tablespoons

Rub this into the grain of a flank steak. Yum!

2 to 3 cloves garlic, finely minced
1/2 teaspoon salt
2 teaspoons cumin
1 teaspoon chili powder
4 teaspoons oil

Mash garlic and salt before combining with other dry ingredients. Stir in oil to form paste.

 TIP: Everyone loves fajitas, but who wants to deal with grilling all those pieces of steak or chicken? Try this. Slather Fajita Rub on flank steak or chicken breasts, cook, then slice thinly. Make fajitas. Enjoy.

SAGE RUB

Yield: 2 to 3 tablespoons

Sage lends an interesting flavor to beef, lamb, pork, and poultry.

2 1/2 teaspoons dried, crumbled sage
1/4 teaspoon minced garlic
2 teaspoons sugar
1 teaspoon salt
2 teaspoons paprika

In a small bowl, mash all ingredients together with the back of a spoon.

MARILYN'S EVERYDAY MIRACLE RUB

Makes about 2/3 cup

This is our "house" rub. It goes well with any meat you're grilling or smoking. We use it on everything from turkey burgers to steak. Make a double or triple batch. Store in a cool place.

$^1/_4$ **cup paprika**
$^1/_4$ **cup packed brown sugar**
1 tablespoon chili powder
1$^1/_2$ teaspoons salt
1 teaspoon minced, dried onion
$^1/_2$ **teaspoon granulated garlic OR garlic powder**
$^1/_2$ **teaspoon black pepper**
$^1/_4$ **teaspoon cayenne powder**

 QUICK RUB TIPS: There are some very
delicious ethnic condiments/seasonings
available in most supermarkets. Have you
tried biryani paste or Thai red curry paste?
Experiment!

SCANDINAVIAN FISH RUB

Yield: About 1/3 cup

Inspired by Gravlax, a cold, cured salmon, this recipe is enough for 1 to 1$^{1}/_{2}$ lbs of any fish filet. Coat the fish with a teaspoon or two of olive oil before applying rub.

3 tablespoons fresh dill, chopped
3 tablespoons brown sugar
1$^{1}/_{2}$ teaspoons coarsely ground black pepper
$^{1}/_{2}$ teaspoon salt

Mash together before rubbing.

Summit Lake,
British Columbia

TOASTED PECAN/ROSEMARY RUB

Yield: Just over ¹/2 cup

We love this on lamb chops, fish filets, or just about anything. Baste whatever you're cooking with a little bit of oil before pressing the pecan rub generously all around.

¹/2 cup pecan halves or pieces
¹/2 tablespoon brown sugar
¹/2 teaspoon ground black pepper
¹/4 teaspoon salt
¹/4 teaspoon ground rosemary

Place nuts on a cookie sheet and bake at 250 degrees for about 10 minutes. Or place them in a skillet on low, tossing a few times, for ten minutes. Let cool. Place nuts in a plastic baggie and crush them with a mallet or hammer until they have a coarse, crumbly texture. Combine with other ingredients.

Marinades

SALMON MARINADE

Makes about 3/4 cup

1/4 cup honey
1/4 cup soy or teriyaki sauce
1 bunch parsley leaves
2 to 3 scallions, trimmed and washed
1/2 teaspoon salt
1 tablespoon dry mustard

Blenderize.

ERICA'S SALMON LACQUER GLAZE

Makes about 3/4 cup

This savory marinade is courtesy of cousin Erica who spent two years teaching English in Japan. We think it translates perfectly!

1/2 cup teriyaki sauce
2 tablespoons sugar
2 tablespoons olive oil
2 tablespoons fresh dill, chopped
1 tablespoon lemon juice
1 clove garlic, finely minced
1 tablespoon wasabi* OR 2 tablespoons
  prepared horseradish
1 tablespoon balsamic vinegar

Combine.

* *Japanese horseradish powder.*

ERICA'S TIP: Baste the fish at least twice during grilling. The marinade gives a crust to the fish as well as a deep mahogany color.

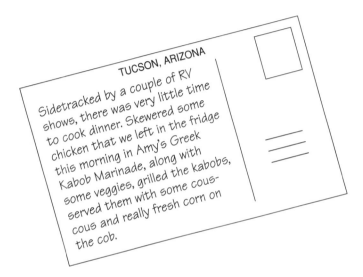

TUCSON, ARIZONA

Sidetracked by a couple of RV shows, there was very little time to cook dinner. Skewered some chicken that we left in the fridge this morning in Amy's Greek Kabob Marinade, along with some veggies, grilled the kabobs, served them with some cous-cous and really fresh corn on the cob.

AMY'S GREEK KABOB MARINADE

Makes about 1¹/4 cups

This marinade sounds disarmingly simple, but once you've tried it with chicken (see recipe, pg. 57) we're sure you'll be using it often.

- **1 cup plain yogurt**
- **Juice of ¹/2 lemon (1 to 2 tablespoons)**
- **2 to 3 cloves garlic, minced or crushed**
- **1 tablespoon oregano**
- **1 teaspoon ground black pepper**
- **¹/2 teaspoon salt**

ORANGE MARINADE #1

Makes about 1 cup

Orange is a great flavor with lamb and beef. It also works wonders on a pork loin, and gives a boost to shrimp and chicken. Why not try it with duck?

6 cloves garlic, minced
2 teaspoons salt
1 6-oz can frozen orange concentrate, undiluted
1/4 to 1/2 teaspoon red pepper flakes
1/4 cup olive or other vegetable oil (optional)

In a small bowl, mash garlic and salt into paste with the back of a spoon. Add juice, pepper, and oil as desired.

ORANGE MARINADE #2

Makes about 1/2 cup

If you don't have orange juice, try this version.

Juice from 1 11-oz can of mandarin orange segments
1 tablespoon olive oil
1/2 teaspoon salt
1/2 teaspoon black pepper
Chipotle or other hot pepper sauce, to taste

Combine. Use orange segments as garnish.

ORANGE MARINADE #3

Makes about 3/4 cup

Here's an orange marinade with a Chinese accent.

1/3 cup soy sauce
2 to 3 tablespoons fresh ginger, minced
2 to 3 tablespoons orange juice concentrate, undiluted
1 tablespoon sugar
2 tablespoons oil

Combine.

ORANGE MARINADE #4

Makes about 3/4 cup

This one has it all!

2 cloves garlic, minced
1/4 teaspoon salt
1 tablespoon fresh ginger
1 tablespoon soy sauce
1/2 cup orange juice
2 tablespoons oil
1 tablespoon sugar
1/4 teaspoon cayenne (optional)

Mash garlic with salt, mash in ginger, and stir in the rest. Or blenderize.

 TIP: Marinades make great side dips! Reserve a bit of any marinade before using. Warm just before serving. If it needs to be diluted, add broth or water. Serve as a sauce alongside your dish.

JERK MARINADE & SAUCE

Makes about 3/4 cup

The jerk, in this case, is a popular Jamaican style marinade. For heat, we've used a fairly conservative amount of cayenne pepper—Jamaicans would use mega-hot scotch bonnet chili peppers. Fiddle with it to your taste. You can double or triple this recipe—if refrigerated, it keeps for about two weeks. This jerk is especially good with chicken and pork.

3 cloves garlic, minced
1 tablespoon fresh ginger, minced
1 medium onion, minced
1 tablespoon brown sugar
1/2 teaspoon black pepper
1/2 teaspoon dried thyme leaves
1/4 teaspoon ground cloves
1/4 teaspoon cayenne pepper
1/4 teaspoon cinnamon
1/4 teaspoon salt
1/8 teaspoon ground nutmeg
Juice of 1 lemon or lime
1/4 cup oil
1/2 teaspoon tamarind paste* (optional)

Mash minced ingredients together, or, even better, puree them in a blender. Combine with the rest of the ingredients.

* This condiment is used in Asian, Caribbean, and other cuisines and can be purchased at specialty food stores. It's very tart, so if you're not using it, add one more lemon or lime to get the right "pucker."

HARMON'S STEAK MARINADE

Yield: About 1/2 cup

A great soak for ribeye steaks or burgers.

1/4 cup teriyaki sauce
1/4 cup water
1 teaspoon balsamic vinegar
1 teaspoon red chile powder
1/2 teaspoon granulated garlic
1/2 teaspoon sugar
1/4 teaspoon curry powder

Combine thoroughly.

IRA'S LAMB MARINADE

Makes about 1 1/2 cups

Ira is justly famous in some parts of upstate New York for his annual pig roast that feeds hundreds. This recipe works well for a smaller crowd.

6 to 10 cloves garlic, crushed
1 teaspoon salt
1 teaspoon black pepper
1 teaspoon rosemary or oregano, crushed
1 cup dry red wine
1/2 cup olive oil
2 tablespoons Dijon mustard (optional)

Mash garlic and seasonings together with the back of a spoon. Add the rest and stir.

Kenai Lake,
Alaska

TIM'S SOY MAGIC MARINADE

Makes about ³/4 cup

The first time we had Tim's chicken we loved it. When
he gave us his marinade recipe we couldn't believe how
easy it was. Now it makes our favorite on-the-road, or
at-home, chicken. You can even start off with frozen
chicken parts. Place them in a plastic baggie with the
marinade, zip it up, and let them thaw while you drive.
Be sure, however, to refrigerate again once the chicken
is thawed. You can also soak the chicken overnight. It
works while you sleep. How nice.

Juice of 1 lemon
¹/2 cup soy sauce
2 tablespoons olive oil

Blend well.

JOHN'S TANGY TURKEY MARINADE

Makes about 3/4 cup

This marinade also makes a mighty tasty salad dressing.

5 tablespoons white wine or other variety of vinegar
1/2 cup olive oil
1 tablespoon ground cumin
1 tablespoon ground black pepper
2 teaspoons garlic, minced
Salt to taste

Combine well and taste for salt before using.

Sauces, Salsas, Chutneys, and More

BBQ BATH

Makes about 1 cup

The essence of BBQ flavors: spicy, sweet, and tangy all at once.

2 tablespoons butter or oil
1 onion, chopped fine
6 to 8 cloves garlic, sliced
1 canned chipotle pepper or other heat, to taste
1/2 cup packed brown sugar or maple syrup
1/4 cup vinegar

In a small pot over medium heat, melt butter, then sauté onion, garlic, and hot stuff. Add sweetener till combined, raise heat, and add vinegar. Bring to a boil, and then reduce heat, cover, and simmer 30 minutes. Use this as a quick dipping sauce with plain grilled chicken.

(YOUR) SIGNATURE BBQ SAUCE

Makes about 3 cups

This one's loaded with our favorite ingredient: garlic. Add your favorite ingredients to make this *your* signature sauce.

1 tablespoon oil
1 small onion, chopped fine
12 cloves garlic, minced fine
1/4 cup balsamic vinegar
1/4 cup packed brown
   sugar
1 tablespoon chili powder
1 teaspoon ground black
   pepper
24-oz plastic bottle of
   ketchup

In a saucepan over medium heat, sauté onions and garlic till very soft. Raise heat, add vinegar, sugar, chili, and pepper. Bring to a boil while stirring. Add ketchup, and stir till it boils. Reduce heat to low, cover, and cook 15 minutes.

 TIP: SAVE THAT KETCHUP BOTTLE! After you've cooked and cooled your sauce, use a funnel to refill the bottle, sign the label, and it really becomes your signature sauce!

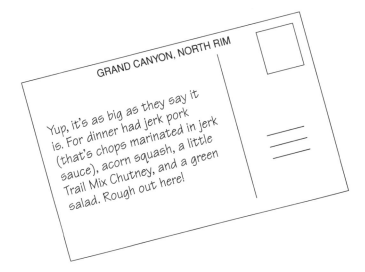

GRAND CANYON, NORTH RIM

Yup, it's as big as they say it is. For dinner had jerk pork (that's chops marinated in jerk sauce), acorn squash, a little Trail Mix Chutney, and a green salad. Rough out here!

TRAIL MIX CHUTNEY

Makes about 2¹/2 cups

Chutney, an Indian-English staple, is a condiment that perks up any grilled dish, but is especially wonderful with lamb or chicken. Store in a tightly covered jar in the refrigerator. Keeps several weeks.

- 1¹/2 cups firm fruit (such as peaches, apricots, pears, apples), diced
- ¹/2 cup packed brown sugar
- 1 tablespoon balsamic vinegar
- ¹/4 teaspoon cumin
- ¹/4 teaspoon cinnamon
- ¹/4 teaspoon black pepper
- ¹/4 teaspoon cayenne pepper
- 1 cup trail mix

Combine and heat all except trail mix; add trail mix when cool.

NO-COOK FRESH FRUIT RELISH

Makes about 1 cup

It's amazing how one or two lonesome pieces of fruit can make a refreshing accompaniment to any meat or chicken dish.

1 cup fresh fruit (such as melon, pineapple, peaches), finely chopped
2 tablespoons maple syrup OR honey OR brown sugar
1 tablespoon lime juice
1 tablespoon Dijon mustard
$1/4$ teaspoon salt
1 teaspoon fresh ginger, minced (optional)

Combine and let sit $1/2$ hour before serving.

SOUTHWESTERN SALSA

Makes about 2 cups

Salsa is, of course, a must with chips, but it is also heaven on a burger or dog, and is great with BBQ chicken.

1 cup chopped tomatoes
  (about 1/2 lb fresh or canned and drained well)
1 teaspoon minced onion
1 clove (1/2 teaspoon) minced garlic
1/4 teaspoon salt
1 teaspoon balsamic vinegar
1 tablespoon chopped fresh cilantro OR parsley
1/2 teaspoon chipotle pepper sauce (optional)
1/2 cup leftover black beans (optional)
1/2 cup leftover corn (optional)

Combine thoroughly. Make double or triple batches. Keeps about one week, refrigerated.

USLI GHEE "TALKING BUTTER"

Makes 1¹/₂ cups

Delicious when used for frying, sautéing, and to top off steamed vegetables, potatoes, or rice.

Usli ghee comes from India and the words literally mean "pure fat." In fact, this is the purest butter—butter that has had all milk solids and excess water removed. Why would you want to do this? Three reasons. First, in the process the butter takes on a delicious nutty flavor. Second, removing the milk solids and water allows the butter to be heated to a higher temperature without burning, so you can fry things like potatoes or cheese sandwiches without scorching them. Third, and most important for camping, it lasts longer. The process is easy, odd, and interesting.

1 lb butter, cut into chunks

In a medium-sized pot, simmer butter over very low heat. When it begins to boil, you'll hear a crackling sound; that's water boiling away. Continue cooking on very low for about 20 to 30 minutes. Just after it stops making noise, the milk solids will start to darken and settle at the bottom of the pot, and the liquid ghee will begin to turn gold and get a slightly nutty aroma. At this point remove it immediately from heat. When it is cool, pour through a sieve into a container with a tight cover. Store in the refrigerator.

SEVERAL SOUPS HOT & COLD

Soup is a favorite, anytime, anyplace. Great for lunch or dinner with salad and bread. Here are a couple of hot ones and a couple of cool ones. They feed a ton of people and the hot ones can be made ahead and frozen.

HOT SOUPS

CABBAGE SOUP

Serves 6 to 8

3 tablespoons butter
1 large onion, chopped
1 small green cabbage, cut in bite-sized chunks
$1/3$ cup flour
3 $14^1/2$-oz cans chicken broth
2 $14^1/2$-oz cans diced tomatoes, preferably with roasted garlic
$1^1/2$ teaspoons sugar

In a large pot over medium high heat, melt butter, and sauté onion till soft. Add cabbage, stir to coat with butter, cook about 10 minutes or till cabbage begins to soften. Sprinkle flour over cabbage and stir to distribute. On high heat add broth, tomatoes, and sugar. Stir. Bring to a vigorous boil, stir, and then reduce heat to low. Cover and simmer 20 minutes.

TIP: If you want to make a hearty supper out of cabbage soup, or make use of yesterday's extras, add any of the following during the last few minutes of simmering, just to heat through: sausages, especially something smoky and garlicky like kielbasa; Meatballs (see pg. 74), and leftover pork chops, deboned and cut in bite-sized pieces.

CHOWDER

Serves 4 to 6

This is a classic chowder. You can make it vegetarian; you can modify the fat by using milk instead of cream; you can make it New England style by adding clams; or you can try the Southwestern additions below. This recipe also can be served cold. Leftovers (if any) can be frozen. How's that for versatile?

1 tablespoon oil or butter
1 large onion, chopped (about 2 cups)
2 large potatoes, peeled and diced (about 2 cups)
1 14-oz can vegetable or chicken broth
1 to 2 cups fresh corn kernels and $1/2$ cup water
  OR 1 14-oz can corn, drained with liquid reserved
$1/2$ cup milk or cream
$1/2$ teaspoon black pepper
$1/2$ teaspoon salt

Heat oil or butter in soup pot over medium heat. Add onions and sauté a few minutes until soft. Stir in potatoes, broth, and corn liquid or water. Cover, bring to a boil, simmer 15 to 20 minutes until potatoes are soft. Add corn and milk (or cream), heat thoroughly, and season. Try adding a few last-minute ingredients to the basic chowder recipe for regional versions.

NEW ENGLAND CLAM CHOWDER

1 6.5-oz can minced clams, with broth
1/2 tablespoon Worcestershire sauce

SOUTHWESTERN CHOWDER

1 jalapeño pepper, diced
4 oz (1 cup) grated cheddar
2 to 3 tablespoons chopped fresh cilantro
1 tablespoon ground cumin

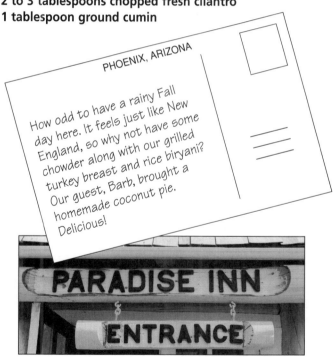

PHOENIX, ARIZONA

How odd to have a rainy Fall day here. It feels just like New England, so why not have some chowder along with our grilled turkey breast and rice biryani? Our guest, Barb, brought a homemade coconut pie. Delicious!

PARADISE INN

ENTRANCE

MAIN COURSE MINESTRONE

Serves 4 to 6

It's fun sometimes to stand over a pot of soup all day, stirring, tasting, adding, and stirring some more. When you want a hearty dish in under an hour, pick through your pantry, as well as your leftovers, and you'll have this rich soup. Don't worry if you don't have some of the ingredients; substitute what you do have. This recipe makes a really hearty soup, the kind that's almost a stew. Serve with plenty of grated parmesan or other cheese on the side, a loaf of bread, and a salad, and you've got dinner. If you prefer a thinner soup, add more broth or water.

> **1 tablespoon oil**
> **1 large onion, chopped**
> **1 cup diced carrots (about 3)**
> **1 cup diced celery (2 stalks)**
> **4 to 6 whole garlic cloves**
> **3 cups chopped tomatoes, fresh or canned with juice (about 1 lb)**
> **4 cups broth OR water OR combination**
> **1 teaspoon dried oregano**
> **1 15-oz can beans, not drained (northern, kidney, navy, or pintos, for instance)**
> **1/2 cup uncooked pasta (preferably small shapes such as orzo, tiny shells, or elbows)**
> **Ground black pepper to taste**
> **Salt, if desired***

Heat oil in a large pot over medium heat. Add onions, carrots, celery, and garlic cloves and stir to coat with oil. Sauté about ten minutes till onions begin to soften. Add tomatoes and broth. Raise heat and bring to a boil, reduce heat to low, cover, and simmer 20 minutes. Add beans, and cook another 10 minutes. Add pasta to the pot and cook according to package directions or to taste. Season to taste.

* *If serving grated parmesan, the cheese will add salt as well.*

BBQ CHICKEN SOUP

Serves 4 to 6

1 tablespoon olive or other vegetable oil
1 large onion, diced
$1/4$ cup flour
1 $14^1/2$-oz can chicken broth, OR vegetable broth
1 $10^3/4$-oz can condensed tomato soup
1 28-oz can diced tomatoes, preferably with roasted garlic
Leftover BBQ chicken, skinned, boned, and cut into chunks
Chipotle pepper or other hot sauce, to taste
Tortilla chips
1 cup shredded cheddar or other cheese

Put oil in large pot over medium heat. Add onion and cook till softened. Sprinkle on flour and stir well. Add broth and soup, raise heat to high, and bring to a boil while stirring. Add chicken and hot sauce. Reduce heat and simmer 10 to 15 minutes. Top with cheese and serve with chips.

COLD SOUPS

Fruit Soups

Serves 6 to 8

Here are a few soups that are as cool to prepare as they are to consume. The basic idea is to have a smooth, slightly thick "broth" with chunks of fruit to be eaten with a spoon. You can garnish your soup with mint leaves, sour cream, or shredded carrots. Serve before the meal or after with a scoop of sherbet.

1 15-oz bag of frozen berries
1 12-oz can frozen juice concentrate (undiluted)
2 to 3 cups fruit salad, with juice, fresh or canned
Juice of 1 lime

The concept is really simple: blenderize or mash the berries, then stir all the ingredients together in a big bowl or pot and serve icy cold.

Appearing below are some fruit combinations you might try.

Fruit	*Juice Concentrate or Nectar*
Blueberries	Pineapple or pineapple/mango/guava
Blueberries	Cranberry
Blueberries	Apple
Raspberries	Lemonade or limeade
Raspberries	Grape
Strawberries	Orange or banana
Strawberries	Apricot nectar
Cherries	Pear nectar

Vegetable Soups

CUCUMBER SOUP

Serves 3 to 5

2 large or 4 medium cucumbers, peeled, seeded, and
   grated or sliced very fine
8 oz sour cream or plain yogurt
1 teaspoon curry powder
$1/2$ teaspoon ground cumin
$1/2$ teaspoon salt

Combine and chill well before serving.

Southern
Utah

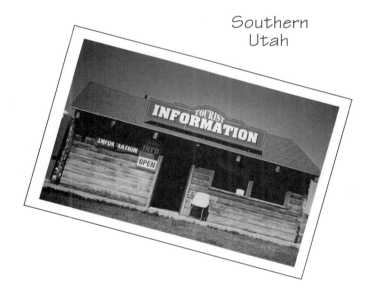

GAZPACHO

Serves 4 to 6

1 14^1/$_2$-oz can diced tomatoes with roasted garlic
1 large or 2 medium cucumbers, peeled, seeded, and diced
1 green bell pepper, seeded, and diced
4 large radishes, diced
Juice of 1 lime
1 tablespoon minced onion
2 tablespoons chopped fresh cilantro OR
   1 teaspoon dried cilantro
^{1}/$_4$ teaspoon salt
1 teaspoon chopped jalapeño
1 cup corn kernels (cooked, canned, or fresh)
1 avocado, diced for garnish (optional)
Sour cream for garnish (optional)

Combine all ingredients through the jalapeño. If
desired, half may be pureed and then recombined with
the rest. Add corn kernels. Chill several hours before
serving. Garnish if desired.

MAINS FROM THE GRILL & SMOKER

TECHNIQUES FOR USING THE GRILL

The principal variables that complicate outdoor cooking are time and heat. Each recipe gives an approximate cooking time. You should fine tune doneness by measuring the internal temperature with an instant-read thermometer (see below). Heat is the variable you need to learn to control or adapt to. The recipes in this book suggest specific temperature settings for grills with built-in thermometers, as well as general guidelines for less sophisticated grills.

Whether or not the grill you are using has a built-in thermometer, here are some useful techniques for controlling the flame/heat levels. Get a covered BBQ. We rarely use the grill without the cover. Although you can broil a steak or burger over the open grill, using the cover prevents grease flare-ups and reduces the risk of spoiling that great piece of meat you bought—or maybe the only thing you have left to eat. Some people want flare-ups to give them the "charcoal blackened" appearance. The "charcoal broiled" taste that we prefer is best achieved by rubbing or marinating the food before grilling.

DETERMINING DONENESS

Some people are able to test for doneness by sticking a fork into whatever they're grilling. If the juices that appear are red, the meat is rare. If the juices are clear, the meat is well done. Others determine doneness by touch. Well-done meat will be firm to the touch, rare will be soft and springy. To be certain of doneness, we use an instant-read meat thermometer to measure the internal temperature. The table on the next page gives you the internal temperatures you'll need to get it right consistently.

Be sure to remove whatever you're cooking from the grill 5 to 10 degrees under the desired final internal temperature. (The meat's internal temperature will rise a bit after it has been removed from the grill.) Then let the meat or poultry rest at room temperature for 5 to 10 minutes before slicing and serving. During this time, the food will finish cooking and the natural juices will settle. The meat or poultry can be loosely covered or tented with foil, but do not cover tightly. If covered, the meat will steam, destroying some of its flavor and appearance.

DESIRED DONENESS	INTERNAL TEMPERATURE AFTER RESTING

(Remove from grill 5 degrees short)

Beef and Lamb

Very rare (bloody)	115 degrees
Rare (red)	120-125 degrees
Medium rare (pink)	125-135 degrees
Medium	135-150 degrees
Well	150-170 degrees

(and for slow-cooked cuts)

Pork

Always cook to at least 138 degrees

Medium	140-155 degrees
Well	155-175 degrees

(and for slow-cooked cuts)

Poultry

White meat	165 degrees
Dark meat	170 degrees

Fish is done when the flesh has turned opaque at the thickest point. Some people enjoy fish cooked rare or medium rare, particularly tuna, swordfish, and other "steak-like" fish. To do this you must judge the doneness by the degree of translucence at the thickest point. Fish cooks very quickly, about 5 minutes per inch of thickness at high heat, so you must remain attentive during the cooking process.

Direct Heat Grilling Method

High Heat. *500 degrees and up.* On a covered charcoal or wood grill, the vents regulate the temperature by controlling the airflow to the fire. The more air, the hotter the fire burns. For high heat, vents should be open and the bonnet will be too hot to touch.

Medium Heat. *300 to 400 degrees.* Open the vents about halfway on a covered charcoal or wood cooker. You will be able to touch the bonnet only briefly.

Slow Heat. *170 to 250 degrees.* Open the vents only slightly, but take care not to smother the fire. You should be able to leave your hands on the bonnet for a few seconds without discomfort.

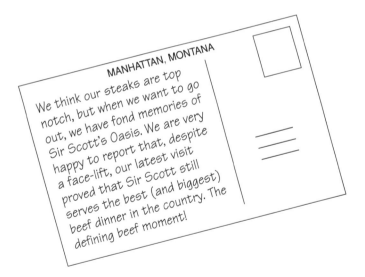

MANHATTAN, MONTANA

We think our steaks are top notch, but when we want to go out, we have fond memories of Sir Scott's Oasis. We are very happy to report that, despite a face-lift, our latest visit proved that Sir Scott still serves the best (and biggest) beef dinner in the country. The defining beef moment!

Indirect Heat Grilling Method

Using indirect heat means the fire is not directly below the item being grilled. If you are using charcoal or wood, the coals are spread to the sides of the grill. If you use gas you can use a drip pan made of foil as a heat defuser. Put it below the cooking grate and directly beneath the item being grilled.

Baking

If you use your grill as an oven to bake, you'll get best results using indirect heat, keeping the heat source to the sides of your food. Some items, such as biscuits, do best when using a two-pan water bath method (using the same principle as a double boiler), to prevent the bottom from scorching. The pan with the food is placed inside one slightly larger pan filled with water.

MAIN COURSES FROM THE GRILL

SENSATIONAL STEAKS

Serves 4

4 New York strip or beef filet steaks cut at least 1" thick (about $1/2$ lb each) OR 2 $1^1/2$" thick steaks, cut in half before cooking
8 tablespoons Marilyn's Everyday Miracle Rub (pg. 21)

Rub steaks on all sides with Marilyn's Rub 1 to 8 hours before grilling. Cover with plastic wrap, refrigerate. Allow meat to come to room temperature before cooking. Grill over hot fire. Turn once. Use instant meat thermometer to be sure of doneness. (Approximate cooking time: 4 minutes for rare, 7 minutes for medium, and 10 minutes for well.)

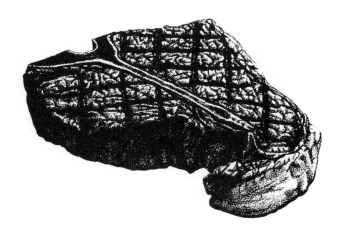

Sequoia National Park

FABULOUS FLANK STEAK

Serves 4

1¹/₂ to 2 lbs flank steak
4 tablespoons Instant Steak Rub (pg. 17) or
Fajita Rub (pg. 20)

Coat steak with rub about 1 to 8 hours prior to grilling. Cover with plastic wrap, refrigerate. Allow meat to come to room temperature. Grill over hot fire, turning once. Use instant-read meat thermometer to be sure of doneness. (Approximate cooking time: 4 minutes for rare, 7 minutes for medium, and 10 minutes for well.)

Remove steak from grill. Allow to rest for 5 to 10 minutes before slicing on the bias in ¹/₄″ thick slices. Arrange on platter and serve.

If you make extra, you'll have great meat the next day for a steak Caesar salad, fajitas, or a Philly cheese steak sub—with plenty of grilled onions and cheddar, please.

LUSCIOUS LAMB CHOPS

Serves 4

8 loin lamb chops 1¹/₂" thick
8 tablespoons C-Rub Plus (pg. 19)

Apply C-Rub Plus 1 to 8 hours before cooking. Cover with plastic wrap and refrigerate Allow to come to room temperature before cooking. Grill over hot fire, turning once. Use instant-read meat thermometer to be sure of doneness. (Approximate cooking time: 8 minutes for rare, 12 minutes for medium, and 15 minutes for well.)

LAZY LEG OF LAMB

Serves 4

1¹/₂ to 2 lbs portion, boned and flattened leg of lamb
3 cups Orange Marinade #1 (pg. 26) or
Ira's Lamb Marinade (pg. 29)

Have butcher bone and flatten a portion of a leg of lamb to prepare it for grilling. Soak lamb in marinade for 2 to 12 hours, covered with plastic wrap, in the refrigerator. Allow to come to room temperature before cooking. Grill over hot fire turning once. Check for doneness at meat's thickest part with instant-read meat thermometer. (Approximate cooking time: 15 minutes for rare, 20 minutes for medium, and 25 minutes for well done.)

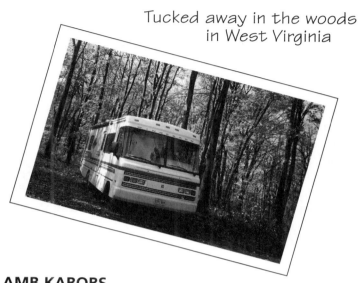

Tucked away in the woods in West Virginia

LAMB KABOBS

Serves 4

1¹/₂ to 2 lbs boneless lamb cubes or steak
1/2 cup C-Rub (pg. 19) or 1 cup Amy's Greek
 Kabob Marinade (pg. 25)

Cut boneless lamb into 1¹/₂" cubes 1 to 4 hours before grilling. Roll cubes in C-Rub or soak in marinade. Cover and refrigerate. Allow meat to come to room temperature before cooking. Skewer meat on 4 stainless skewers leaving narrow spaces between cubes. Grill over hot fire turning 4 times. (Approximate cooking time: 5 minutes for rare, 8 minutes for medium, and 12 minutes for well.)

JUICY PORK CHOPS

Serves 4

4¹/₂ lbs loin chops cut about 1" thick
8 tablespoons Happy Pork Rub (pg. 17) or ¹/₂ cup
Jerk Marinade (pg. 28)

Rub or marinate 1 to 8 hours before cooking. Cover with plastic wrap and refrigerate. Allow to come to room temperature before cooking. Grill over hot fire. Turn once. Use instant-read meat thermometer to be sure of doneness. Pork must be cooked to at least 138 degrees Fahrenheit to kill any parasites, but we prefer the meat cooked to medium well, or an internal temperature of 155 degrees (approximate cooking time 15 minutes).

On the
Alaska Hwy

TENDER PORK LOIN

Serves 4

1¹/₂ to 2 lbs pork loin
6 tablespoons Country Pork Rub (pg. 18)

Apply rub 1 to 8 hours before cooking. Cover with plastic wrap and refrigerate. Allow meat to come to room temperature before cooking. Grill over hot fire. Turn once. Use instant-read meat thermometer to be sure of doneness. Pork must be cooked to at least 138 degrees (F) to kill any parasites, but we prefer the meat cooked medium well, or to an internal temperature of 155 degrees (approximate cooking time 15 minutes). Allow meat to rest, cut into ¹/₄″ slices on the bias, and serve.

TANTALIZING TURKEY

Serves 4

1¹/₂ to 2 lbs boned turkey breast filets
¹/₂ cup John's Tangy Turkey Marinade (pg. 31)

Soak turkey covered with plastic wrap in refrigerator for 2 hours. Turn once to coat each side. Allow meat to come to room temperature before cooking. Grill over medium hot fire (about 450 degrees) for about 15 minutes, turning once. Check internal temperature with an instant-read meat thermometer for doneness. Allow to rest for 5 minutes before slicing on the bias and serving.

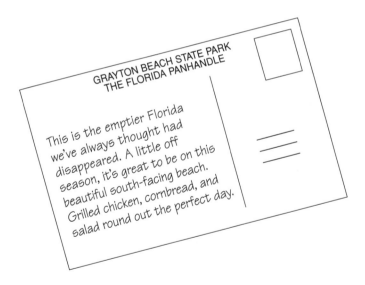

GRAYTON BEACH STATE PARK
THE FLORIDA PANHANDLE

This is the emptier Florida we've always thought had disappeared. A little off season, it's great to be on this beautiful south-facing beach. Grilled chicken, cornbread, and salad round out the perfect day.

THE BEST GRILLED CHICKEN

Serves 4

3 lbs chicken parts, with skin and bones
2 cups Tim's Soy Magic Marinade (pg. 30)

Soak chicken in Tim's Magic for 1 or more hours.
Cover and refrigerate. Bring to room temperature.
Cook over medium fire (about 350 degrees), turning 4
times. Check for doneness with instant-read
thermometer (cooking time
approximately 50 minutes).
Make extra and you'll have
a great portable lunch the
next day.

AMY'S GREEK CHICKEN KABOBS

Serves 4

1¹/₂ to 2 lbs boneless chicken cut in chunks
1 recipe Amy's Greek Kabob Marinade (pg. 25)
1 medium onion, cut in chunks
1 red bell pepper (or some green and yellow too),
  seeded, cored, and cut in chunks
8 mushrooms

Skewer pieces, alternating the chicken and vegetable
chunks for variety and color. Soak, covered and
refrigerated, for at least 1 hour in Amy's Greek Kabob
Marinade. Allow meat to come to room temperature
before cooking. Baste grill with oil before cooking.
Cook over medium heat (350 degrees), turning 4 times.
(Approximate cooking time: 30 minutes.)

GRILLED SALMON STEAKS

Serves 4

4 salmon steaks, 1" thick
3/4 cup Erica's Salmon Lacquer Glaze (pg. 24)

Soak the fish in the marinade, covered, in the refrigerator at least one hour before grilling. Allow salmon to come to room temperature. Grill over hot fire, turning and basting at least once until slightly firm and opaque in the center (about 4 minutes in total).

AMY'S FISH PACKETS

Serves 4

1/4 cup mayonnaise
1 tablespoon honey mustard OR 1 tablespoon prepared hot
mustard OR 1 tablespoon horseradish
1 teaspoon dried dill
1/2 teaspoon garlic powder
4 fish filets, about 1" thick (about 1 1/2 lbs)

Have ready 4 large pieces of foil. Combine first four ingredients and spread on fish. Make loose packets. Chill one hour. Grill 10 minutes.

USING THE GRILL AND A SMOKER BOX

Smoked Main Courses

WONDROUS RIBS

Serves 4

2¹/2 lbs country-style pork ribs
3 tablespoons Country Pork Rub (pg. 18)
3 cups hickory wood chips

Soak wood chips in water for 2 or more hours. Apply Country Pork Rub 1 to 12 hours before cooking, cover with plastic wrap, and refrigerate. Allow meat to come to room temperature before cooking. Fill smoke box with 1$1/2$ cups soaked hickory chips. Arrange ribs on grill. Cook over slow fire (about 250 degrees), turning once. Refill smoke box after 1 hour. Check for doneness with instant-read meat thermometer. (Approximate cooking time: 1$3/4$ hours.)

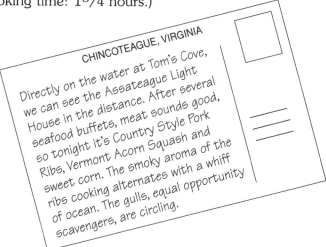

CHINCOTEAGUE, VIRGINIA

Directly on the water at Tom's Cove, we can see the Assateague Light House in the distance. After several seafood buffets, meat sounds good, so tonight it's Country Style Pork Ribs, Vermont Acorn Squash and sweet corn. The smoky aroma of the ribs cooking alternates with a whiff of ocean. The gulls, equal opportunity scavengers, are circling.

SMOKED CHICKEN

Serves 4

3 lbs chicken thighs (or your favorite parts, bone in)
2 cups hickory wood chips

Soak wood chips in water 2 hours or more before using. Place 1 cup soaked wood chips in smoke box and arrange on grill with chicken parts. Cook over slow fire (about 200 degrees). Turn chicken once and refill smoke box after 1 hour. Check for doneness with instant-read meat thermometer. (Approximate cooking time: $1^3/4$ hours.)

 TIP: Leftover smoked salmon or chicken, minced and mixed with some mayonnaise and served on crackers, makes very elegant nibbles before dinner.

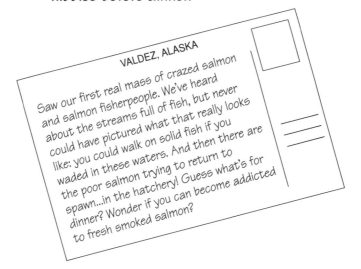

VALDEZ, ALASKA

Saw our first real mass of crazed salmon and salmon fisherpeople. We've heard about the streams full of fish, but never could have pictured what that really looks like: you could walk on solid fish if you waded in these waters. And then there are the poor salmon trying to return to spawn...in the hatchery! Guess what's for dinner? Wonder if you can become addicted to fresh smoked salmon?

SMOKED SALMON

Serves 4

**1¹/₂ lbs salmon filet about ³/₄" thick at center,
  OR 4 steaks, ³/₄" thick
1 recipe Salmon Marinade (pg. 24)
  OR Erica's Salmon Lacquer Glaze (pg. 24)
1 cup hickory wood chips**

Soak wood chips in water 2 hours or more before using. Place salmon in the marinade to soak 1 to 8 hours before cooking, cover and refrigerate. Allow salmon to come to room temperature before cooking. Place soaked wood chips in smoke box and arrange on grill with salmon, skin side down. For steaks, turn once and baste several times. Cook over slow fire (about 200 degrees). (Cooking time: approximately 45 minutes.)

MAIN COURSES ON A BUN
(OR A PLATE IF YOU PREFER)

HAPPY HAMBURGERS

Serves 4

1¹/₃ lbs ground chuck
8 tablespoons Marilyn's Everyday Miracle Rub (pg. 21)

Form ground chuck into 3/4″ thick patties, handling as little as possible. Apply Marilyn's Everyday Miracle Rub, cover with plastic wrap, and refrigerate. Allow meat to come to room temperature before cooking. Grill over hot fire. Turn once. Use instant-read meat thermometer to be sure of doneness. (Approximate cooking time: 4 minutes for rare, 7 minutes for medium, and 10 minutes for well.) Serve on hamburger buns, your favorite roll, or a slice of hearty bread, toasted slightly.

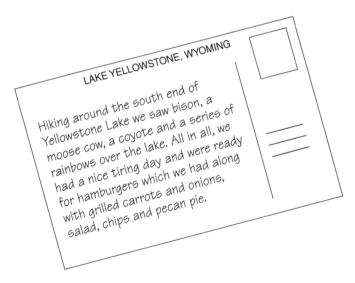

LAKE YELLOWSTONE, WYOMING

Hiking around the south end of Yellowstone Lake we saw bison, a moose cow, a coyote and a series of rainbows over the lake. All in all, we had a nice tiring day and were ready for hamburgers which we had along with grilled carrots and onions, salad, chips and pecan pie.

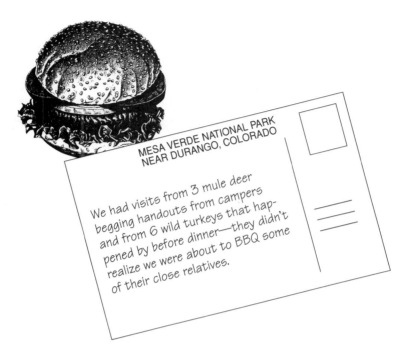

MESA VERDE NATIONAL PARK
NEAR DURANGO, COLORADO

We had visits from 3 mule deer begging handouts from campers and from 6 wild turkeys that happened by before dinner—they didn't realize we were about to BBQ some of their close relatives.

TASTY TURKEY BURGERS

Serves 4

1¹/2 to 2 lbs ground turkey
8 teaspoons Harmon's Steak Marinade (pg. 29)

Form ground turkey into 3/4″ thick patties . Place in marinade for 1 hour in refrigerator, turning once. Allow turkey to come to room temperature before cooking. Grill over medium-hot fire. Turn once. Use instant-read meat thermometer to be sure of doneness. (Approximate cooking time: 10 minutes for well.) Serve on hamburger buns, your favorite roll, or a slice of hearty bread, toasted slightly. You can top these with tomatoes and pickles, just like regular burgers, or try them with cranberry sauce or Trail Mix Chutney (pg. 33).

SAUSAGE SPECIALS

Serves 4

Among our favorites is Aidell's Smoked Turkey & Chicken Sausage with sun-dried tomatoes.

2 lbs (about 8 links) precooked sausage

Grill the sausage over a hot fire until brown and heated through. Serve on a hot dog bun or your favorite hearty bread with mustard, sauerkraut, shredded cheese, Roasted Whole Peppers (pg. 102), and a side of Cucumber Salad (pg. 105).

COEUR D'ALENE, IDAHO

We drove on into Idaho to spend the night and BBQ some of the food we picked up yesterday in Seattle. We had fresh corn, homemade sausages of various kinds, couscous, salad, and ice cream. We deserved a good meal. And another hot tub.

⑷ INDOOR MAINS

Be prepared—it works for the Boy Scouts! If it looks like rain, grill enough for two meals, throw a few sausages on for tomorrow's pasta, or get creative with leftovers in a stir fry. Even if it's gloomy outside, it will be warm, cozy, and aromatic inside. We had the best time making pasta and steaming up all the windows while we were trying to keep warm at Blueberry Lake, near Johnson Pass in Alaska—in July!

Food really does taste better while camping. Lucky for the chef. That also means you can loosen up and combine foods you might not otherwise get away with, such as serving a meal without veggies or with three veggies. Generally everyone is so happy and so hungry, as long as it's tasty and there's enough of it, your efforts will be well received.

All the recipes in this chapter are also geared to being prepared ahead or at the very last minute, as in the case of the stir frys. That way the chef doesn't have to miss out on any of the fun hikes or other activities!

ON REHEATING

Microwave, covered with plastic wrap, vented, 3 to 5 minutes.
Bake, covered with foil, vented, at 400 degrees for 20 to 30 minutes, inside or outdoors.
Stir fry, on high for a minute or two.

ABOUT STIR FRYING

To "stir fry" means to cook lots of chopped or small things over high heat very quickly, while shoving them around to avoid burning. A wok or large pan and a long handled spoon or non-stick spatula are the only tools you need. The preparation—gathering, sorting and chopping—actually takes longer than the cooking itself. Stir frying is also a great way to use leftovers since lots of ingredients can be combined. For instance, how else could you make good use out of an ear of corn, three shrimp, a leftover pork chop, and one lonesome scallion? Sounds like fabulous pork fried rice! We generally like to combine the starch (rice or noodles) with the other ingredients. You may prefer to serve them side by side.

SOUTHERN ITALIAN PASTA

Serves 4 to 6

This is a toothsome main dish. It's best with short, dense pasta such as ziti, penne, rigatoni, or even elbows.

1/2 lb pasta
1 tablespoon olive oil
4 Italian hot or sweet sausages (about 3/4 lb)
14-oz jar tomato sauce
1/2 cup parmesan cheese, grated
1 cup mozzarella, shredded
1 teaspoon hot pepper sauce, mixed into sauce (optional)
1/4 cup cream, mixed into sauce (optional)
1/2 teaspoon crushed sage or rosemary (optional)

Cook pasta 1 minute less than package directions. Drain, return to pot, and toss with olive oil. To cook sausage, prick each several times, then either microwave on a plate with paper toweling for 4 minutes or pan fry till firm. Slice to be sure there are no raw sections. Cool a bit and slice. Combine pasta, sausage, and three-fourths of sauce. Spread remaining sauce in bottom of oven/microwave proof 6"x10" or 7"x11" baking dish. Add half the pasta, half of each cheese, remaining pasta, and top with remaining cheeses. Microwave, loosely covered with plastic, for 7 minutes, or bake at 450 degrees, loosely covered with foil, about 30 minutes.

 TIP: THE COOKING TENT. To keep foil or plastic wrap away from melting cheese, support with several toothpicks, forming a tent.

WILLIAMS, ARIZONA

Imagine our surprise when we stopped at about 6PM to spend the night and had to watch the nice man plow a foot of snow out of our campsite before we could drive in! Tonight is the coldest we've spent in the RV; at last report it was 14 degrees! Glad to have a great big dish of steaming pasta and sausage on a night like this.

NORTHERN ITALIAN PASTA

Serves 4

A very quick dinner served warm or an excellent cold lunch a day or two later. Best with crusty bread and a green salad.

$1/2$ lb pasta
$1/4$ cup olive oil
15-oz can great northern or cannelini beans,
   drained and rinsed
1 cup green beans, cooked, cut in bite-sized pieces
1 garlic clove, peeled and mashed with $1/2$ teaspoon salt
Parmesan, grated
1 to 2 cups leftover vegetables, cut in bite-sized pieces
   (optional)
Roasted Whole Peppers (pg. 102), roughly chopped (optional)

Cook pasta according to package directions. Drain and toss with remaining ingredients. Serve parmesan on the side.

AROMATIC PASTA

Serves 4

$^1/_2$ lb short pasta
2 tablespoons olive oil
2 to 3 cups leftover smoked chicken or ham, diced
1 large onion, chopped
$^1/_2$ lb mushrooms, sliced
$^1/_2$ cup parmesan, grated
$^1/_2$ cup dried porcini mushrooms, reconstituted in $^1/_2$ cup
  cream, milk, broth, water, OR dry wine (optional)
$^1/_2$ teaspoon rosemary, dried and crushed (optional)

Preheat oven to 400 degrees. Cook pasta one minute less than package directions. Drain, toss with 1 tablespoon oil, and combine with meat. Place other tablespoon of oil in pan over medium high heat. Sauté onion and mushrooms until soft. Add to pasta. Stir in cheese and optionals. Bake, covered, for 20 minutes.

McCarthy, Alaska

CAJUN STIR FRIED RICE DINNER

Serves at least 4

1 tablespoon oil
1 large onion, chopped
2 stalks celery, chopped
1 red or green bell pepper, chopped
2 cloves garlic, chopped
1 bay leaf
1 tablespoon paprika
1 teaspoon salt
1 teaspoon black pepper
$1/2$ teaspoon thyme
$1/4$ teaspoon cayenne pepper
About 3 cups of leftover shrimp, chicken, sausage
    OR combo, cut to bite size
1 recipe Rice (pg. 91), cooked, cooled, and fork fluffed
    to separate grains
1 14-oz can stewed tomatoes, drained
Hot sauce (optional)

In large wok or frying pan, heat oil over high heat. Stir fry vegetables until they are browned. Reduce heat to medium, and stir in spices. Add leftover meat/seafood. Stir to mix. Add rice. Stir to mix. Add tomatoes. Turn heat to high and heat through.
Remove bay leaf.

Flaming Gorge, Utah

ASIAN RICE

Serves 4

2 tablespoons oil
1 to 2 cloves garlic, minced
1 tablespoon fresh ginger, minced
2 to 3 cups leftover pork, beef, chicken, shrimp
   OR combo, diced; OR 1 package firm tofu, drained, dried
   on paper toweling, sliced, dried again, and diced
1 recipe Rice (pg. 91)
3 to 4 tablespoons soy sauce
2 scallions, chopped (optional)
1/2 cup bean sprouts (optional)

In large wok or frying pan heat oil; sauté ginger and garlic in the oil for 30 seconds. Add leftovers or tofu. Stirring constantly, add rice. When rice begins to brown, add soy and combine well. Garnish with scallion or bean sprouts, if desired.

TIP: BUG OFF! To keep the bugs off your food while you're prepping, cover with cutting boards, plates, or upside-down bowls or pots.

COUSCOUS CURRY

Serves 4

If you're not familiar with couscous (pronounced kooskoos), head for the rice section of your market and pick up a box. It's a wheat product made from semolina flour, just like pasta, and is formed into tiny grains. The best part is that it requires no cooking, only standing in boiling water. The variations are endless. Have fun.

1 5.8-oz package couscous
2 to 3 cups leftover chicken OR lamb, diced
1/2 cup leftover vegetables OR thawed frozen peas OR diced carrots
1/2 cup raisins
1 tablespoon curry powder
1/4 cup unsalted cashews, slivered almonds, or other nuts

Prepare couscous according to package directions. Add meat, vegetables, and curry powder. Reheat as needed. Garnish with nuts. Serve with Trail Mix Chutney (pg. 33).

Wild Ponies
Bite and Kick
Keep Your Distance
Do Not Feed

SHEPHERD'S PIE

Serves 6 to 8

A sturdy English pub standard. Served with a selection of pickles and relishes, it's a complete meal.

1 tablespoon oil
1 medium onion, chopped
2 cloves garlic, minced
1 to 2 carrots, peeled and diced
1^1/$_2$ lbs ground meat
^{1}/$_2$ teaspoon salt
^{1}/$_2$ teaspoon ground black pepper
^{1}/$_2$ teaspoon dried thyme
3 tablespoons dry sherry OR 1 tablespoon
   Worcestershire sauce and 2 tablespoons water
2 tablespoons flour
Mashed Potatoes (pg. 89)
^{1}/$_2$ cup shredded cheddar cheese (optional)

Preheat oven to 400 degrees. In large pan or wok over medium heat, heat oil and sauté onion, garlic, carrots and meat until no pink is left. Season, add liquid, sprinkle on flour, and then raise heat and stir constantly till thickened. Spoon meat mixture into 6″x10″ or 7″x11″ Pyrex dish. Spoon and spread potatoes (and cheese) on top. Cover with foil and bake 20 minutes. Remove foil, and bake another 10 minutes.

MEATLOAF / MEATBALLS

We use the same basic recipe for either meatballs or meatloaf. Sometimes the loaf has a heart of cheese (whatever kind's around) or a lid of bacon strips. The sauce for the meatballs varies depending on our mood and pantry items. Some ideas follow.

BASIC LOAF/BALLS

Serves at least 6
with plenty of leftovers

1 carrot, peeled and finely chopped
1 small onion, finely chopped
1 stalk celery, finely chopped
2 tablespoons water
1/2 cup bread crumbs OR 2 slices white bread
   OR 1 dinner roll OR 1 hamburger or hot dog bun
1/2 cup milk or water
1/2 teaspoon salt
1/2 teaspoon black pepper
1/4 teaspoon oregano
1/4 teaspoon thyme
1/4 teaspoon rosemary, crushed
2 lbs ground meat (beef, pork, turkey or any combo)
1 teaspoon olive oil

Place vegetables and 2 tablespoons water in microwavable container. Cover loosely and cook 3 minutes on high, or steam in a pot for 3 minutes. Drain. Meanwhile, soak bread/crumbs in milk. Combine vegetables, soaked bread, and seasoning. Taste and adjust seasoning before adding meat. Add meat and combine gently by hand to avoid toughening the meat. (This should require no more than 15 to 20 motions.)

Form loaf (5"x 9"x 2^1/2" pan) OR about 40 1^1/2" balls OR 1 smaller loaf and 20 balls.

To cook balls: Heat oil in wok or skillet over medium heat. Cook until light brown all over and firm, or about 10 minutes. Reduce heat to low, cover, continue cooking 15 minutes longer. Remove from pan if you're going to make sauce in it.

To make loaves: Preheat oven to 400 degrees. Place in 5"x 9"x 2$\frac{1}{2}$" loaf pan. Cover with foil. Bake 45 minutes. Uncover and bake an additional 15 minutes to brown. Let sit 5 to 10 minutes before slicing.

Some ideas for meatball sauces: Meatballs are always good in tomato sauce, but if you want to try something different, here are some suggestions. First, remove meatballs from the pan and set aside. Then, with pan on medium heat, add 1 tablespoon flour and stir to blend with juices. Add one of the following combinations.

- 2 tablespoons Dijon mustard, $\frac{3}{4}$ cup cream, 1 teaspoon caraway seeds
- 1 cup sautéed mushrooms and onions, $\frac{3}{4}$ cup dry red wine
- $\frac{3}{4}$ cup beef broth, $\frac{1}{2}$ teaspoon crushed rosemary
- 2 teaspoons dried onion soup mix, 3/4 cup water, $\frac{1}{2}$ teaspoon black pepper

Bring to a boil, lower heat and simmer a few minutes.

 TIP: What to do with those zillions of extra hot dog or hamburger rolls? Freeze and use them here or in other recipes that call for bread crumbs.

TURKEY ROLL-UPS

Serves 2 to 3

Turkey parts are available everywhere. The question is what to do with them. Here's one answer.

**1 lb boneless, skinless turkey breast, cut into
   long thin slices**
1/4 lb ham, salami or prosciutto, sliced thin
**1/2 to 1 cup dried fruit (raisins, apples, pitted prunes),
   diced fine**
1 to 2 tablespoons oil

Cover each slice of turkey with ham. At narrower end, place fruit. Roll up as tightly as possible. Hold together with wooden toothpicks, if necessary. Heat pan over medium heat, add oil and turkey. Sauté until all sides are browned and meat is cooked through and no longer pink when sliced. Serve on a plate or in a bun.

CAMPFIRE CHILI CON CARNE

Serves 8 to 10

This dish has as many versions as there are campers and cowpokes. In New Mexico, "chile" means a sauce made of chile peppers, either red or green. If you want both, it's called Christmas. Neither has meat, tomatoes, or beans. In Texas, "chili" is made with chunked, not ground, meat. Ours has both kinds of chiles, uses chopped meat, and is beanless. If you prefer beans, either add a 15-oz can of drained pintos to this recipe or serve Western Beans (pg. 84) on the side. If you keep your eye on the pot and stir from time to time, chili can simmer for several hours either indoors or out. Leftover or frozen and reheated, it just seems to get richer and better tasting.

1 tablespoon oil
1 large onion, chopped
6 cloves garlic, mashed
2¹/2 lbs ground or chopped beef OR half pork/half beef
¹/2 to ³/4 cup red chile powder
2 14¹/2-oz cans diced tomatoes with roasted garlic
1 7-oz can chopped green chiles
¹/2 cup chopped fresh coriander
**   OR 1 tablespoon dried cilantro leaves**
2 tablespoons dried oregano
1 tablespoon ground cumin
Cayenne pepper OR chipotle pepper sauce to taste
Salt to taste

Heat oil in a large pot over medium heat. Add onions and sauté, stirring until clear and soft. Add garlic and meat. Stir until all pink color is gone. Raise heat to high, add chile powder, tomatoes, and chiles, and bring to a boil. Stir from the bottom up, then add remaining ingredients, except salt. Reduce heat to low, and cover. Simmer at least an hour, stirring from time to time. Salt to taste just before serving.

Chili Sides

Just as chili itself is unique to the chef, everyone has their favorite ways to serve it. Here's how we do it up.

Musts

Rice
Western Beans (pg. 84)
Flour or corn tortillas or tortilla chips

Options

Shredded cheddar or jack cheese
Chopped fresh tomatoes
Shredded iceberg lettuce or leaves of romaine
Sour cream
Chopped onions
Chopped fresh cilantro
Chopped jalapeño chiles

CHILI TORTA

Serves 1 or 2

Here's an idea for using leftover chili. Along with a salad, and perhaps some rice and beans, this makes a quick supper.

3 large flour tortillas
1 cup chili
2 slices ham or turkey
2 slices cheddar, jack, or other cheese
Jalapeño chiles as desired

In a microwavable or baking dish layer tortillas, chili, meat, cheese, tortilla, and so on, ending with a tortilla. Microwave for 2 to 3 minutes or bake at 400 for 15 minutes, until heated through. Cut in wedges.

 TIP: To degrease a pan in a hurry, hold the food back with a fork or spatula, and carefully tip the pan to one side. Place a crumpled paper towel or napkin in the side where the grease pools. Remove paper carefully and discard. Repeat, tilting the pan the other way.

On the
Alaska Hwy

SMILE, BUCKLE
YOUR SEAT BELT
and make the
best of it!

Yukon

SPAGHETTI PIE

Serves 4 to 6

An old favorite. Many years ago a recipe for spaghetti pie was copied over and over again and passed around Marilyn's office. At first, it sounded so unlikely, but as we tried it, we became converts. Here's how we make it on the road today.

2 eggs
1/2 cup grated parmesan cheese
1/2 lb thin spaghetti
1 tablespoon olive oil
1 large onion, chopped (about 1 cup)
2 cloves garlic, minced
1 large bell pepper, chopped
Hot pepper (optional)
3/4 cup sour cream OR ricotta cheese
   OR cottage cheese OR some combination
3/4 lb (about 3 links) Italian sausage (hot or sweet)
1 cup tomato sauce OR 1 6-oz can tomato paste
   and 3 tablespoons water
1 cup (4 oz) shredded mozzarella

Preheat oven or grill to 400 degrees. In medium bowl, beat eggs and parmesan. Cook pasta 1 minute shy of package directions, drain, and add to egg/cheese mixture. Place in 10″ Pyrex pie plate to form shell. Next, sauté onions, garlic, and pepper till soft. Combine with sour cream and spread in pie shell. Then remove sausage from casings, crumble into pan, and cook till no longer pink. Discard grease. Add tomato sauce and bring to a boil. Pour into pie.

Cover with foil and bake 20 minutes. Uncover, sprinkle with mozzarella, raise heat to 500, and bake another 10 minutes till browned. Let it cool at least five minutes before trying to slice. This can be microwaved, but won't have the same crispy "crust."

ORANGE SHRIMP

Serves 2 or 3

A light flavorful dish that will make you think you're sitting on the beach in Mexico. Or maybe you are! Serve with plenty of rice.

- **1 tablespoon oil**
- **1 medium onion, chopped (about 1 cup)**
- **1/2 cup orange juice**
- **2 to 3 tablespoons fresh cilantro, chopped**
- **$^1/_2$ teaspoon salt**
- **1 lb shrimp, peeled and cleaned**

Heat oil in a medium frying pan, add onions, and sauté until soft. Raise heat to high and add juice, cilantro, and salt. Bring to a boil and reduce to low. Add shrimp and stir as shrimp turn pink.

⬟(5) SIDES

In our minds, sides can be as interesting as the main event. How often have we ordered the chicken or the chop just because it came with the garlic mashed potatoes or onion rings that made us salivate? Sound familiar? Read on.

These sides are meant to be as tasty as they are easy. Most can be part of a great "salad bar" lunch the following day.

MAGGIE'S GREEN BEANS

Serves 4

    4 strips bacon, chopped
    1 small onion, chopped
    1 lb green beans, fresh or canned, drained
    1 14.5-oz can tomatoes

Sauté bacon and onion on stovetop or in microwave. Add beans and then tomatoes and stir. Cook on stovetop, covered, 20 minutes if using fresh beans, and 10 for canned. In the microwave, cook 15 minutes if using fresh beans, and 5 minutes for canned.

WESTERN BEANS

Serves 4 to 6

1 Italian sausage (about 1/4 lb)
1 15-oz can pinto or other beans, drained, liquid reserved
1 1/2 teaspoons ground cumin
1 cup shredded cheddar cheese (optional)
1 jalapeño pepper, sliced (optional)

Remove sausage from casing, crumble into pan, and cook over medium heat. When no longer pink, add beans and mash with the back of a fork until beans are as smooth as you like. Add liquid as needed to form puree. Heat through. Add cumin. Garnish with cheese and pepper before serving.

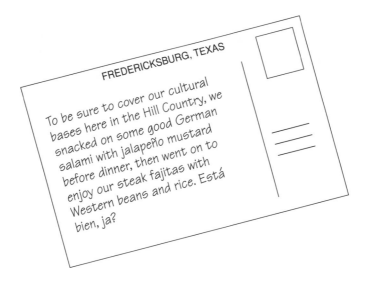

FREDERICKSBURG, TEXAS

To be sure to cover our cultural bases here in the Hill Country, we snacked on some good German salami with jalapeño mustard before dinner, then went on to enjoy our steak fajitas with Western beans and rice. Está bien, ja?

EASTERN BEANS

Serves 3 to 4

3 strips bacon, chopped into pieces
1/4 cup chopped onion
1 teaspoon Dijon or other hot mustard
1 tablespoon maple syrup OR molasses
   OR brown sugar OR honey
1 15-oz can great northern or other beans, drained

Sauté or microwave bacon until done. Cook onions with bacon till wilted. Add mustard, syrup, and beans. Heat thoroughly.

GINGER BROCCOLI

Serves 2 to 4 (depending
on size of broccoli)

You can adapt this recipe for most vegetables. Consider using carrots, asparagus, or summer squash. Keep in mind that harder vegetables must be cooked longer.

1 bunch broccoli (florets and chopped stems)
2 cloves garlic, minced
1 tablespoon ginger, minced
1 tablespoon soy sauce
1 tablespoon olive oil

Combine all, cover, vent, and microwave on high 4 minutes. On the stovetop, first steam or boil broccoli 5 to 10 minutes, drain, and then add remaining ingredients and simmer together 5 more minutes.

VERMONT ACORN SQUASH

Serves 2 to 4

These flavors remind me of our family Thanksgivings in Vermont, but the recipe works well everywhere. In addition, uncooked acorn squash keeps really well unrefrigerated, and does not seem to mind the bumpiest of roads.

1 medium sized acorn squash
2 tablespoons maple syrup OR brown sugar OR honey
$1/2$ teaspoon salt
$1/4$ teaspoon cinnamon
$1/8$ teaspoon cayenne pepper
Dash ground nutmeg
Butter to taste

Wash and prick squash with a fork or knife to allow venting. Microwave 10 to 15 minutes on high or bake at 400 for 30 minutes. Let sit until cool enough to handle. Slice open and discard seeds. Divide remaining ingredients between the two halves and reheat, if needed. OR after baking and removing seeds, remove all flesh to a bowl, combine with remaining ingredients, and mash.

GARLIC GREENS

This works with green beans, broccoli, or leafy greens such as chopped chard, collard, or mustard.

¹/₂ to 1 cup vegetable per serving
¹/₂ tablespoon butter per serving
¹/₂ teaspoon fresh chopped garlic per serving

Steam veggies for 3 minutes. Drain off water completely. Sauté garlic in butter or microwave for 30 seconds. Add greens, toss, and heat.

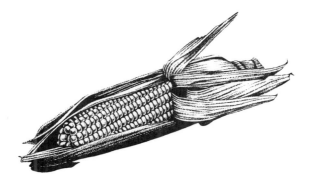

CORN ON THE COB

Serves 2

We always pick up fresh corn when we come across it. This method of preparing it was shown to me by a very clever lady named Carole.

2 ears corn, husked

Rinse corn, do not dry, and place in zip lock bag. Vent the bag, removing as much air as possible. Microwave on high for five minutes, turning once.

HOT BUTTERED POPPING CORN

Serves 4

When you can't get good fresh corn, try this unique method of pan "roasting."

1 15-oz can corn (try to find a brand without sugar to avoid scorching)
1 tablespoon butter
1/2 teaspoon salt

Drain, rinse, and dry corn on paper towels. Heat large frying pan or wok over high heat. Place dry corn in dry pan, spreading it out evenly. Without stirring, wait till the corn pops a few times. Then stir to get the corn somewhat browned, but not blackened. Turn off heat, stir in butter and salt.

Canyon de Chelly
National Monument

MASHED POTATOES

Serves 4

Everyone loves mashed potatoes and they needn't be off the charts in terms of calories.

**1¹/2 lbs potatoes (4 small, 3 medium, or 2 large),
    peeled, cut in large chunks**
**1 scant cup buttermilk OR milk OR cream OR broth
    OR a combination of liquids, at room temperature**
¹/2 teaspoon salt
¹/2 teaspoon black pepper
1 tablespoon butter

Boil potatoes for about 20 to 25 minutes, or till fork tender (not mushy). Mash till lump-free or put through ricer. Slowly add milk till potatoes reach the consistency you favor. Add salt. Top with butter.

 TIP: Plain mashed potatoes are getting all dressed up these days. You may want to try one of these additions: 4 cloves roasted garlic (peeled, baked slowly till soft), a tablespoon or two of horseradish, a handful of grated parmesan or cheddar cheese, or a chopped, sautéed onion.

MARILYN'S FAMOUS LOW-FAT BAKED STUFFED POTATOES

Serves 4

2 medium baked potatoes (about 1 lb)
$1/2$ cup buttermilk
$1/4$ teaspoon ground cumin
$1/4$ teaspoon salt
$1/4$ teaspoon ground black pepper
2 oz low-fat cheddar cheese, cut in four chunks
2 tablespoons grated parmesan cheese

Preheat oven or grill to 450 degrees. As soon as potatoes are cool enough to handle, cut in half lengthwise. Without breaking the skins, scoop potatoes into a small bowl. Mash with a fork and add milk and seasonings. Potatoes should be fluffy, but not at all runny. Refill skins halfway, and then place one piece of cheddar in each, top the cheese with remaining potatoes, and round off the tops with a spoon. Put parmesan on a small plate and gently roll potato tops in cheese to coat. Place on foil or foil-lined metal sheet. Bake 20 minutes, until tops are nicely browned.

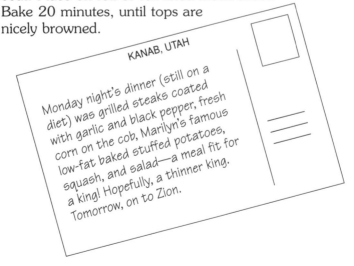

KANAB, UTAH

Monday night's dinner (still on a diet) was grilled steaks coated with garlic and black pepper, fresh corn on the cob, Marilyn's famous low-fat baked stuffed potatoes, squash, and salad—a meal fit for a king! Hopefully, a thinner king. Tomorrow, on to Zion.

RICE

This is the tastiest and most reliable method we've found for cooking rice.

1 cup long grain or basmati rice
1 14-oz can broth plus 2 tablespoons water or butter
  OR 2 cups water

Place rice and liquid in glass dish. Cover with plastic, vent. Microwave 15 minutes. Stir with a fork to separate grains.

On the stovetop, place all ingredients in a covered pot. Bring to a boil. Reduce heat to simmer. Total time comes to 15 minutes.

 TIP: While this recipe has more flavor than most, you might want to zip up your rice even more. Before cooking stir in one of the following: 2 tablespoons pesto, 2 tablespoons biryani paste, or 2 tablespoons tomato sauce or paste. If it's heat you're looking for, how about salsa, hot sauce, chipotle sauce, or chili paste? Start off with tiny amounts (^{1}/2 teaspoon) and work up to your taste/heat level.

FRIED RICE

Serves 4

This needs to cook fast and hot. Using a non-stick spatula is helpful to push the rice around so it will cook without burning (see About Stir Frying, pg. 66).

- **2 tablespoons oil, plus another 2 tablespoons as necessary, preferably peanut or neutral tasting**
- **1 medium onion, chopped OR 4 scallions, chopped**
- **1 tablespoon fresh ginger, chopped**
- **3 to 4 tablespoons soy sauce**
- **2 to 3 cups cold, cooked rice (pg. 91), grains separated with fingers or fork if the rice has become a solid mass in the cooling process**

In a wok or large frying pan heat oil over high heat, sauté onions and ginger one minute, and add rice. Using the spatula, move rice around so all sides fry. Add more oil as necessary to moisten and prevent sticking. When rice begins to get brown and crispy, add soy, and stir until well distributed.

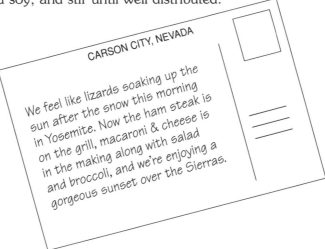

CARSON CITY, NEVADA

We feel like lizards soaking up the sun after the snow this morning in Yosemite. Now the ham steak is on the grill, macaroni & cheese is in the making along with salad and broccoli, and we're enjoying a gorgeous sunset over the Sierras.

MACARONI & CHEESE

Serves 4 as a main course,
6 as a side

Everyone smiles when you say "macaroni and cheese,"
don't they?

   1/2 lb macaroni or other short pasta
   1 tablespoon oil
   2 tablespoons butter
   1 large onion, chopped
   2 tablespoons flour
   2 cups milk OR 1 12-oz can evaporated milk
      and 1/2 cup water
   1 teaspoon salt
   1/2 teaspoon black pepper
   1/8 teaspoon cayenne powder
   1 teaspoon dried sage, oregano, or other herb, to taste
   8 oz (2 cups) sharp cheddar cheese, shredded

Preheat oven to 400 degrees. Cook macaroni two
minutes less than package directions. Drain, and toss in
oil to prevent sticking. To make the sauce, sauté onion in
butter over medium heat till soft. Reduce heat. Sprinkle
with flour, stir to combine thoroughly. Let bubble gently
for about one minute. Raise heat to high, add liquid
while stirring, and bring to a boil. Reduce heat to low.
Season, add cheese, and stir till sauce is smooth. Do not
let sauce boil once cheese has been added. Fold pasta into
sauce, place in buttered, ovenproof 7"x 11" dish. Bake,
uncovered, until bubbly and brown (about 30 minutes).

 TIP: SAVE THAT SAUCE! This sauce recipe
makes about 3 cups. You can freeze 1 cup for
later to use on 1/4 lb of pasta or vegetables.
Pour over toast to make delicious Welsh
rarebit for lunch!

TIP: Marilyn's mother used to put buttered crumb topping on lots of things, and for good reason: it was a major enticement for children to eat vegetables they weren't so crazy about. But buttered crumbs are also great on macaroni and cheese. Melt 2 tablespoons butter, and combine with $1/2$ cup crumbs. Sprinkle before baking. Or you can crush a handful of crackers, such as Triscuits, to top off your mac & cheese.

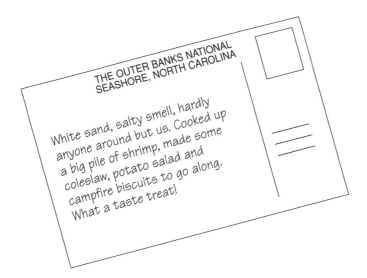

THE OUTER BANKS NATIONAL SEASHORE, NORTH CAROLINA

White sand, salty smell, hardly anyone around but us. Cooked up a big pile of shrimp, made some coleslaw, potato salad and campfire biscuits to go along. What a taste treat!

SIDES ON THE GRILL

CAMPFIRE BUTTERMILK BISCUITS

Makes 8

2 tablespoons powdered buttermilk reconstituted
   in $^1/_2$ cup cold water OR $^1/_2$ cup buttermilk
1 cup all-purpose flour
$^1/_2$ tablespoon baking powder
$^1/_3$ teaspoon salt
3$^1/_2$ tablespoons cold butter

Preheat grill to medium-high heat, about 425 degrees.
If necessary, reconstitute powdered buttermilk with
water; set aside. Combine dry ingredients in a bowl and
mix with fork. Add cold butter cut into $^1/_4''$ slices. Cut
in butter with 2 knives or pastry cutter—the mixture
should resemble coarse meal. Do not overmix; lumps of
butter are okay. Add buttermilk and stir a few times
with a fork until ingredients form a powdery ball. Drop
heaping tablespoons of dough into a cast iron skillet
that will fit in your BBQ. Alternately, drop dough into a
9"x 6" disposable aluminum
pan. Place this pan into a
second 9"x 6" disposable
aluminum pan with $^1/_4$
cup water. Cook over
medium, indirect fire
for 15 to 20 minutes,
until golden brown.

CHEF BILL'S CAMPFIRE POTATO PACKETS
Serves 4

We learned how to make this tempting dish from a great chef and teacher, Bill Weiland. When you open these packets, the side-by-side stacks of potatoes, oozing with cheese, butter and spices, are irresistible.

4 medium boiling potatoes, cooked till just tender
1 teaspoon salt
1 teaspoon ground black pepper
2 medium cloves garlic, finely chopped
1 tablespoon onion, finely chopped
1 teaspoon jalapeño pepper, finely chopped
4 oz (1 cup) cheddar cheese, crumbled
2 tablespoons butter, cut in 8 pieces

Arrange 4 1-ft pieces of aluminum foil. Cut each potato in $1/4''$ thick slices. In a small bowl or cup, combine seasoning ingredients. Begin each packet by placing two slices of potato side by side on the foil. Continue layering spices, cheese, potato, placing butter and spice on top. Close foil to seal packets. Heat for 20 minutes over a medium-low fire, about 300 degrees, turning once.

 TIP: Packets can be grilled along with other food. If your fire is hot, reduce potato cooking time to 12 minutes. Turn each packet 4 times. Also, most grills will have hot and cool spots—use the cool spots for campfire potatoes.

CAMPFIRE HOME FRIES

Serves 2

2 small potatoes, about ¹/₂ lb
2 small onions
2 teaspoon oil
1 teaspoon Marilyn's Everyday Miracle Rub (pg. 21)

Peel and cut potatoes in large chunks, or quarter smaller potatoes. Skin and quarter onions. Boil potatoes 10 minutes, add onion, and boil for another 5 minutes. Drain. Toss in oil, and sprinkle with seasoning. Place on vegetable rack over medium-hot fire. Turn once or twice, cooking 15 minutes, until golden brown and crispy.

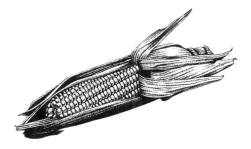

ROASTED CORN

Serves 4

4 ears fresh sweet corn on the cob
2 tablespoons soft butter
Salt and pepper (optional)

Carefully peel back the husks, but don't remove them. Discard the silks. Apply the butter and season. Carefully replace the husks to cover corn. Soak in cold water one hour. Grill over hot fire for about 20 minutes, turning 4 times. Remove from grill, and peel and discard husks. Serve hot.

CORNBREAD

Yield: 10 to 12 wedges

This works well on the grill. Make sure the cover can close over your skillet!

1 cup cornmeal
1/4 cup flour
1/2 teaspoon salt
1/2 teaspoon baking powder
1/2 teaspoon baking soda
2 eggs, lightly beaten
1 cup (or 1 8.5-oz can) creamed corn
1 cup sour cream OR buttermilk OR combination
1/2 cup oil or 1 stick melted butter
1 7-oz can diced green chiles, drained
2 to 4 strips of bacon, chopped, cooked,
  including grease (optional)
1 chopped onion (optional)
1 to 2 seeded and chopped jalapeño peppers (optional)
1 tablespoon oil

Preheat oven or grill to 425 degrees. In a large bowl combine dry ingredients. Separately, mix all other ingredients except 1 tablespoon oil, and then combine wet and dry. Heat 10″ cast iron skillet over high heat on stovetop or on preheated grill. Swirl in reserved oil to coat bottom and sides. Pour in batter. After a minute or two, crust will begin to form. Bake 20 minutes (or 30 minutes over 5,000 feet), or till toothpick, fork, or skewer comes out clean.

☞ TIP: DON'T TOUCH THAT! Despite a thorough hand washing, oils from hot peppers can stay on your skin for many hours. Always use gloves or put plastic bags over your hands when working with hot peppers. And please, don't take your contact lenses out any time soon either. We know. We've tried.

Keuka Lake State Park, New York

VEGGIES FROM THE GRILL

Here's something you can do with just about every vegetable. Large ones go right on the grill, smaller ones (asparagus, garlic cloves, cherry tomatoes) are cooked in a "basket" made for this purpose available in kitchen stores, hardware stores, or by mail.

Grilled veggies are excellent the next day, chilled, at room temperature, or reheated. Or chop and toss with your favorite dressing as a salad.

Preparing to Grill Veggies

Slice vegetables and peel as desired.

Coat with oil, sprinkle with salt and let sit $1/2$ to 2 hours in a bowl, bucket, baggie, etc.

Have ready long-handled spatula, fork, tongs, hot mitt, and serving platter.

Plan on using the entire grill surface for vegetables before you prepare the rest of your meal.

Tips for Grilling

Sort veggies by similar size and hardness, which determine cooking time. Cook over medium-high heat. Keep lid on between turning to prevent flame-ups. Turn frequently. Spread out on large platter or tray when done. Cover loosely with foil.

Serving Notes

Serve at room temperature. You may want to season with salt, pepper, and a bit of crushed rosemary.

What to Cook

Asparagus
Carrots, sliced lengthwise
Zucchini, sliced lengthwise
Large onions, cut in rounds
Eggplant (requires repeated basting with oil)
Tomatoes, cut in half or in thick slices across
Turnips
Potatoes
Sweet potatoes
Broccoli
Peppers, sliced

SANTA BARBARA, CALIFORNIA

Tonight we are at El Capitan
State Park. We are out in the
woods, beside a brook, grilling
veggies, filet mignon and
campfire potatoes. It feels good
to be out of the city. Tonight is
the full moon so we are on the
alert for signs of magic.

ROASTED WHOLE PEPPERS

We love these. And it's so much fun to burn something on purpose. (Really, they have to be blackened in order to shed their skins.) A savory side dish or tasty addition to pasta, rice, sandwiches or salads, these keep in the fridge for several weeks.

3 large, firm red, yellow or other bell peppers, whole, rinsed and dried

You can skewer them for easy turning or have two long-handled tools or tongs handy to do the job. Roast over an open fire until they are charred all over. Place in a paper bag or cover loosely with foil or an upside-down pot or bowl to steam while they cool. The peppers will be very soft.

Remove blackened skins as follows: Hold peppers under running water or in a large bowl filled with water. Peel off charred skin with your fingers. Discard skin, stems, and seeds.

Tear or slice peppers into strips. Place in flat container or dish. Toss with the following ingredients.

1 to 2 tablespoons olive oil
Salt (optional)
Pepper (optional)
Balsamic vinegar
   (optional)
Garlic, sliced
   (optional)

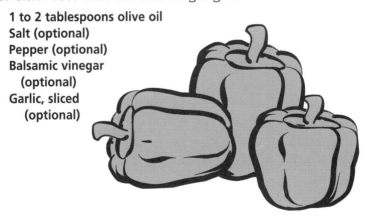

6 SALADS & DRESSINGS

SALADS

Slaw 101

Good basic slaw is hard to come by, but easy to make. Here are the fundamentals.

Grate raw cabbage, red or white, or a combo. Knead the grated cabbage a bit to soften it before dressing with Slaw Dressing (pg. 111). Best if left to sit, covered and refrigerated, 2 to 24 hours, before eating.

CARROT/APPLE SLAW

Serves 4

2 large carrots, peeled and shredded
1 tablespoon lemon juice
1 Granny Smith apple, peeled, cored and shredded
1/2 cup plain yogurt OR mayonnaise OR combo
1/4 cup raisins
1 teaspoon honey or sugar
Salt
1 teaspoon fresh ginger, grated
1/2 cup chopped nuts (optional)

Combine carrots and lemon, grate apple, and add quickly to avoid browning. Toss remaining ingredients, and season to taste.

PINK SALAD

Cool, crunchy and very colorful.

1 cup pickled beets, drained, chopped
1 15-oz can chick peas, drained
1 cucumber, peeled, seeded, and diced
3 to 4 tablespoons sour cream, OR yogurt, OR mayonnaise
1 tablespoon fresh herb such as dill, chopped
Salt (optional)

Combine, toss, and chill.

BROCCOLI (OR OTHER VEGETABLE) SALAD

1 recipe Ginger Broccoli (pg. 85)
2 tablespoons mayonnaise

When cool, add mayonnaise and toss.

CORN SALAD

Serves about 6

2 to 4 ears leftover corn, cut from cob
1/4 cup Whole Roasted Peppers (pg. 102), chopped
   OR 1/2 cup bell peppers, chopped
1 to 2 stalks celery, sliced
1 15-oz can chick peas, drained and rinsed
1 tablespoon chopped fresh
   OR 1 teaspoon dried herb
   such as basil, parsley, cilantro,
   oregano or sage (optional)
1/2 minced jalapeño pepper (optional)

Toss with desired amount of Our House Dressing (pg. 110).

CUCUMBER SALAD

Serves about 6

Cool, a little sweet, a bit of heat.

2 cucumbers, peeled,
   cut in half lengthwise,
   seeded and sliced
1 recipe Thai Style
   Dressing (pg. 112)

Combine and let sit, refrigerated, at least several hours before serving.

JOHN'S MOM'S KANSAS FARM
POTATO SALAD

Serves 4 to 6

This is the best we've ever had. Remember to boil the potatoes until just done and let them cool thoroughly before dicing.

1/2 cup mayonnaise
2 tablespoons dill pickle juice
2 tablespoons white vinegar
1 stalk celery, diced fine
1/4 cup minced onion
2 dill pickles, diced fine
1 hardboiled egg, chopped
1 lb boiling potatoes (2 or 3), peeled, boiled,
  cooled, and cubed
Salt to taste

Stir mayonnaise, pickle juice, and vinegar till smooth. Add celery, onions, pickles, and egg. Salt to taste. Gently fold in potatoes and chill.

 TIP: John, and probably his Mom, would hate this, but sometimes we add a spoonful of Dijon mustard or a small chopped tomato.

SWEET POTATO SALAD

Serves 8 to 10

Here's an unusual salad that came about as the result of what we had in the kitchen at dinnertime one night. What a lucky coincidence of ingredients!

2 to 3 lb sweet potatoes, peeled, and diced to 1" cubes
1 cup water
1 recipe Yogurt Dressing (pg. 113)
1/2 cup unsalted peanuts

Microwave potatoes in water, covered, and vented, for 10 minutes on high, or simmer on the stovetop about 15 minutes. Stir and test for doneness. Cook more, if necessary. Drain and let cool. Toss with Yogurt Dressing. Refrigerate. Garnish with peanuts just before serving.

 TIP FOR DRYING LETTUCE: Salad spinners are a nice idea, but we don't have the space for one. So we let gravity dry the salad for us. Place washed lettuce in a clean, dry towel or pillow case. Step outside and spin it around your head. With vigor. Or place towel-wrapped lettuce in a plastic grocery bag and let 'er rip indoors. Nice dry salad, no extra utensils.

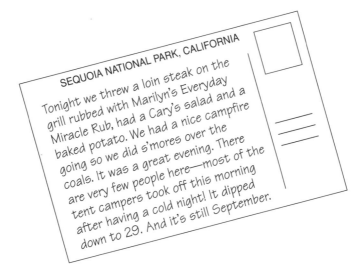

SEQUOIA NATIONAL PARK, CALIFORNIA

Tonight we threw a loin steak on the grill rubbed with Marilyn's Everyday Miracle Rub, had a Cary's salad and a baked potato. We had a nice campfire going so we did s'mores over the coals. It was a great evening. There are very few people here—most of the tent campers took off this morning after having a cold night! It dipped down to 29. And it's still September.

CARY'S SALAD

Serves 4

Many years ago in Manhattan our neighborhood restaurant, Cary's, used to serve a salad that inspired this version at home and on the road. It's a slightly sweet/tangy/savory/crunchy thing.

1/4 cup olive oil
1 to 2 tablespoons balsamic vinegar
1/2 teaspoon salt
1/4 teaspoon ground black pepper
1 Granny Smith apple OR other type of apple
    OR crisp pear, cut in bite-sized slices
4 handfuls romaine lettuce, washed and dried,
    cut into pieces
2 to 3 tablespoons crumbled blue cheese
1/3 cup toasted pecans

In a salad bowl, combine oil, vinegar, salt, pepper, and apple. Toss in lettuce. Top with cheese and nuts.

CAESAR DINNER SALADS

These are great when the weather's hot, or served with soup when it's chilly. You can make a vegetarian meal out of this salad, or use up leftover meats, or grill chicken breasts, a small steak, or your favorite fish to slice and place on top of the salad.

1 head romaine lettuce, cut, washed and dried
   (one large handful per serving)
Caesar Dressing (pg. 106)
Meat, fish, or chicken, if desired
Croutons, if desired

In a large bowl, toss lettuce with desired amount of dressing. Top with meat or fish, or croutons, as desired.

On the
Alaska Hwy

SALAD DRESSINGS

OUR HOUSE DRESSING

Makes about 2¹/₂ cups

6 to 8 cloves garlic, minced
¹/₂ tablespoon salt
2 cups olive oil
¹/₄ cup balsamic or raspberry vinegar
   OR regular vinegar and 1 teaspoon sugar
Black pepper
Hot sauce to taste

Mash garlic and salt, and then add other ingredients, or blenderize. This dressing keeps, refrigerated, for several weeks.

CAESAR DRESSING

Makes about 2 cups

This luscious version of the classic contains no eggs and keeps, refrigerated, for several weeks.

1¹/2 cups olive oil
3 cloves garlic, minced
2¹/2 tablespoons lemon juice (about 1 lemon)
1 tablespoon anchovy paste (about half of a 1.6-oz tube)*
1/2 cup parmesan cheese, grated
1 tablespoon ground black pepper
1/2 tablespoon Worcestershire sauce
Salt to taste

Shake or blenderize all ingredients except salt. Add salt to taste.

* *Anchovy paste can be found in the canned fish section of most supermarkets. It really gives this dressing an authentic flavor.*

SLAW DRESSING

Makes about 3/4 cup

1/2 cup mayonnaise
1 to 2 tablespoons vinegar OR lemon juice
Buttermilk OR milk OR water to thin mayonnaise,
 if necessary
Salt and black pepper

Combine dressing ingredients. Use immediately.

THAI STYLE DRESSING

Makes about 3/4 cup

1/4 cup sugar
1/4 cup boiling water
1/4 cup white vinegar
1/4 teaspoon red pepper flakes
Chopped cilantro (optional)
Salt (optional)

Mix sugar in water till combined. Add other ingredients. This dressing keeps well.

MT. RANIER, WASHINGTON

After a beautiful, but tough day hiking, it's back to our campfire and time to BBQ our dinner. Tonight's menu: grilled pork chops, roasted new potatoes, acorn squash and a salad in ginger east-west dressing. Just the end of another really tough day on the mountain.

BARBARA'S EAST/WEST DRESSING

This makes a tasty dressing for chicken salad and is excellent on leftover green beans, broccoli, peas, and other vegetables. It's so easy, yet everyone will ask you for the recipe. Ready?

Mayonnaise
Soy sauce
Fresh ginger, minced

Combine in proportions that taste good to you.

YOGURT DRESSING

Makes about 2 cups

1¹/₂ cups plain yogurt
1 tablespoon honey or maple syrup
¹/₄ cup raisins
3 tablespoons seeds, some combination of flax, sunflower, sesame, poppy, among others
¹/₂ teaspoon salt

Combine.

PEANUT DRESSING

About 3/4 cup

If you like Chinese sesame noodles, this dressing has a very similar taste. Use it to make a cold pasta salad. Garnish with cucumber slices, minced scallion greens, and a bit of chopped fresh cilantro or parsley.

1/4 cup chunky peanut butter
1/4 cup warm water
1/4 cup soy sauce
1 tablespoon sugar
1/4 teaspoon salt
1/4 teaspoon red pepper flakes

Dissolve peanut butter in water. Add other ingredients.

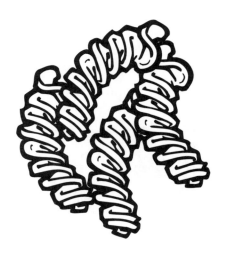

⑦ DESSERTS

Confession time. On the road we are not big bakers—we're more into assembling desserts, especially after dinner around the old campfire. Herewith our favorites.

"A" IS FOR ANGEL FOOD CAKE

Angel food is the happy camper's secret weapon at dessert time. You can find perfectly good angel food cake in most grocery stores and the ways to dress it up are unlimited. Here are some starter ideas.

MAKE YOUR OWN INSTANT PINEAPPLE UPSIDE-DOWN CAKE

Serves 8 to 10

1 angel food cake, sliced
1 pineapple, diced into bite-sized chunks
   OR 1 can pineapple chunks, with juice or syrup
1 to 1^1/$_2$ cups toasted pecans*
1 to 1^1/$_2$ cups pecan or maple syrup,
   at room temperature or warmed

* *Toast pecans in a 250 degree oven for about 10 minutes.*

Distribute the cake, plates, and forks. Pass the rest around as toppings.

RED DEVIL ANGEL FOOD CAKE

Serves 4

1 pint strawberries, washed, hulled,
   and sliced the long way
1/4 cup sugar
2 tablespoons orange juice or water
1 1/2 tablespoons orange, OR almond, OR vanilla extract
4 slices angel food cake

Toss first four ingredients together. Cover and let sit in a cool place for an hour or more so there will be lots of juice. Spoon over angel food cake slices.

APRICOT ANGELS

Serves 4

1/2 cup apricot jam
1/4 cup dried apricots OR raisins, chopped
2 tablespoons almond OR vanilla
   OR rum OR brandy extract
1/2 cup toasted slivered almonds
Vanilla ice cream
4 slices angel food cake

Combine jam, fruit, and liquid, and heat for 45 seconds in microwave or two minutes in a small saucepan just before serving. Pour over sliced cake, and top with nuts and ice cream.

ANGEL S'MORES

Serves 4

1/2 cup dark chocolate fudge sauce, warmed
1/4 cup marshmallow creme
4 graham crackers, 8 halves
4 thin slices angel food cake

For each portion, stack and spoon as follows: cracker, sauce, cake, sauce, marshmallow, cracker. Squeeze together to make a sandwich. Say "aaahhh."

RASPBERRY RAVE

Serves 8 to 10

1 1-lb bag frozen raspberries, thawed
1/2 cup sugar
1 cup dark chocolate fudge sauce, warmed
1 angel food cake sliced in half horizontally

Assemble this just before you need it. Combine berries and sugar. Heat until sugar dissolves. Let cool. Pour half the mixture over the bottom half of the cake, and follow with a tunnel of half the chocolate. Replace the top of the cake, and then spoon the remaining fruit on top, allowing for plenty of drips. Drizzle the remaining chocolate over the fruit.

TROPICAL INTERLUDE

Serves 4

1 cup chopped fruit such as banana, pineapple, mango,
   papaya or any combo, with juices
1/4 cup dark rum OR
   fruit juice
1/4 cup marshmallow
   creme
4 slices angel food cake
1/2 cup shredded coconut

Combine fruit and liquid.
Spread each slice of cake
with marshmallow and
fruit, and sprinkle with
coconut.

ORANGE ANGEL

Serves 4

1 11-oz can mandarin oranges
   OR 2 oranges, peeled, sectioned, with juice
Honey or maple syrup
4 slices angel food cake
2 to 3 tablespoons sesame seeds

Mix fruit, juice, and honey or syrup. Pour over slices of
cake; top with loads of sesame seeds.

Sweet Tooth Emergency Rations

Here are some other items you may want to keep on hand for "A" cake or other last-minute sweet cravings/emergencies.

Chocolate chips, chunks, syrup, or bars
Fruit syrups, maple syrup, honey, butterscotch toppings
Nuts, nut butters, peanut butter chips
Canned, fresh, or dried fruit
Ice cream, whipped cream, yogurt
Sweetened condensed milk
Marshmallows

Good luck and please report any major news in the "A" cake department to us!

Dessert Sandwiches

Dessert sandwiches are a camping classic. Herewith the original and some variations.

S'MORES

Marshmallows
Graham crackers
Chocolate bars

Have ready graham crackers broken in half, every other half topped with a piece of chocolate. Toast marshmallows over the campfire. Press hot marshmallow between crackers to melt the chocolate. Eat immediately.
Make s'more.

FUDGE S'MORES

Okay, here's a real sweet tooth pleaser. Instead of using chocolate bars, use slices of your homemade fudge (next page) when making s'mores. MMMMMM.

PEANUT BUTTER AND JELLY COOKIES

An indoor s'more.

Graham crackers
Peanut butter
Jam/jelly

6-MINUTE FUDGE

This dessert is a quick version of a classic with seven flavor variations. Since the base mixture becomes very hot and bubbles up, please use a large, deep (at least 8 cups or 2 quarts) ceramic or glass bowl suitable for microwaving. On the stovetop, use a deep pot and instead of timing, use a standard candy thermometer, and cook till soft ball stage or 236 degrees, if you are at sea level or thereabouts.

 NOTE: Boiling temperature will decrease about 2 degrees per thousand feet, so at 5,000 feet aim for 226 degrees, and at 10,000 feet quit at 216 degrees. If you're not sure where you are, boil water and see what the temperature is. At sea level it would be 212 degrees Fahrenheit.

FUDGE BASE

1 14-oz can sweetened condensed milk
1 stick ($^1/_2$ cup or $^1/_4$ lb) cold butter

Place ingredients in large, deep glass or ceramic microwavable bowl. Microwave on high for 3 minutes. Stir until well combined and smooth. Microwave again for 3 minutes on high. Stir until well combined again. The mixture should be slightly darker and quite thick. Before flavoring, let cool slightly so that you can touch the bowl comfortably, but the mixture is still warm enough to melt the chips.

Additions to Flavor Fudge

First, stir in items to be melted with a rubber spatula, and then fold in nuts and other additions.*

* Chips seem to be packaged in odd lot quantities. We have found 8, 10, 11, and 12 oz versions. The smaller amounts are given in these recipes, but you can also use the larger ones.

Chocolate Fudge

Stir in 1 8-oz package chocolate chips.

Rocky Road Fudge

Stir in 1 8-oz package chocolate chips. Fold in $1/2$ cup chopped marshmallows or miniatures and $1/2$ to $3/4$ cup chopped walnuts or other nuts.

Peanut Butter Fudge

Stir in 1 6-oz package peanut butter chips. Stir in $1/2$ cup unsalted peanuts, if desired.

Coconut Fudge

Stir in 1 8-oz package white chocolate chips. Fold in 1 3.5-oz can sweetened shredded coconut.

Coffee Fudge

Spoon a little of the hot fudge base into a small dish or cup. Stir in 3 tablespoons instant espresso or other finely ground instant coffee until it's evenly incorporated. Recombine with base. Add one package (8 to 12 oz) white chocolate chips. Stir till combined and smooth.

Mocha Fudge

Spoon a little of the hot fudge base into a small dish or cup. Stir in 1 to 2 tablespoons instant espresso or other finely ground instant coffee until it's evenly incorporated. Stir in 1 8-oz package chocolate chips.

Key Lime Fudge

Stir in 1 package (10 to 12 oz) white chocolate bits. Add the grated zest of 2 small limes and the juice, as desired.

Forming the Fudge

There are several ways to handle this. You can spread the mixture in a disposable aluminum pan either 8" x 8" or 6" x 9", or in a buttered glass or metal pan. Or form a log on a double thickness of aluminum foil, and then roll up tightly for slicing. Or make individual balls.

Refrigerate overnight. Can be wrapped in foil or placed in covered containers. This fudge can be frozen, and keeps for weeks.

Kenai Lake, Alaska

OTHER FAVORITE DESSERTS

BROWNIES

Makes 16 1" squares

Everyone has their favorite recipe. Here's ours. We're warning you: they're very fudgy.

1 12-oz bag chocolate chips
1 stick soft butter (1/2 cup or 1/4 lb)
2 eggs, lightly beaten
1 cup flour
1/2 teaspoon baking powder
1/4 teaspoon salt
1 cup nuts, coarsely chopped (optional)

Preheat oven or grill to 350 degrees. Melt chips in the top of a double boiler or in a large bowl in a microwave for 2 1/2 minutes. (Be sure to check if they're melted by stirring; they hold their shape deceivingly well.) Stir in butter till combined, followed by beaten eggs, and then dry ingredients and nuts, if any. Pour into buttered 8" x 8" baking dish. Bake 25 minutes. Cool, and then refrigerate several hours before devouring.

 TIP: When buttering cake pans, use the paper from your softened butter. Enough butter usually adheres to the paper to do the job and you won't feel like a grease monkey afterwards.

ICE CREAM PIE

This is another house favorite. The "work" involves 8 minutes of crust baking. Once you've got that crust, the assembly choices are endless.

Ice Cream Pie Crust

1 9-oz package Nabisco Famous Chocolate Wafers
1/2 cup sugar, brown or white
4 oz (1 stick) melted butter

First, turn the oven to 350 degrees. Crush the cookies. If you have a food processor handy, use the steel blade and whirl the cookies till crumbled. If you don't, place the cookies in a zip lock or other heavy plastic bag. Close tightly, removing air, and then double bag. Crush cookies by hand, foot, or whack them with a rolling pin. It's fine to leave bits the size of chocolate chips. Stir in the butter and sugar. Press cookie mixture into a 9″ pie plate. Bake 8 minutes. Cool before filling.

Filling

2 pints ice cream, slightly softened

Optional Toppings

Whipped cream
Marshmallow creme
Sprinkles
Chocolate or other chips
Crushed nuts

After filling and topping, pie should be frozen at least one hour before serving.

BANANAS PRUDHOE

Serves 4

As if to prove eating well is portable, Mary invented these while camping with her husband, Dan, at Prudhoe Bay, Alaska, which is pretty close to the edge of the world.

  2 tablespoons brown sugar
  1/4 cup cream OR half-and-half
  1 tablespoon butter
  1/2 teaspoon ground cinnamon (optional)
  2 tablespoons white flaked coconut (optional)
  2 tablespoons rum (optional)
  2 firm bananas, peeled, cut in half, then in half lengthwise
  Several slices of lime (optional)

In a small dish or cup, combine sugar and cream and set aside. Melt butter in a frying pan over medium heat. Pour sugar/cream mixture into bubbling butter. Stir constantly until clear and carmelized. Reduce heat to low. Add any of the options at this point, and then add bananas, spooning carmelized mixture over the bananas as they warm. Serve on a nice plate, and garnish with limes if desired. Serve along with a hot cup of coffee or tea.

BANANA BREAD

Makes 1 loaf

This qualifies as dessert (especially when warm and topped with vanilla, or better yet, banana, ice cream), but can also be used to make great cream cheese and raisin sandwiches.

2 large eggs
3 bananas, very ripe and mushy
1 cup firmly packed brown sugar
2 cups buttermilk or buckwheat pancake mix
**   OR 2 cups flour, 1 teaspoon baking powder,**
**   1 teaspoon baking soda, and 1 teaspoon salt**
1 cup chopped pecans or walnuts
1/4 teaspoon cinnamon

Butter a 9"x 5"x 3" loaf pan. Preheat oven to 350. Combine ingredients, and pour into loaf pan. Bake about 45 minutes, or until toothpick comes out clean.

Somewhere in the West

DESSERT ON THE GRILL

Yes, ladies and gentlemen, you can make dessert on the grill. Here are a few, we hope, inspiring ideas.

GRILLED FRUIT

Grilling fruit enhances its flavor by carmelizing its sugar, thereby intensifying its natural sweetness. As when grilling vegetables, it's wise to sort fruits by firmness, which generally dictates the amount of cooking time they'll require. Canned fruits, such as peaches and pear halves and pineapple slices, can be placed directly on the grill. Small firm fruits, such as fresh pineapple chunks, apple quarters, and unripe banana chunks, should be skewered.

> **1 cup fruit per person**
> **2 tablespoons neutral cooking oil**
> **Cinnamon, nutmeg, brown sugar, or toasted coconut
>   for sprinkling after cooking (optional)**

Assemble and sort fruit by firmness. Pat dry with paper towel. Lightly coat fruit with oil. Skewer smaller, harder fruits. Grill fruits of like firmess together over hot fire while turning 3 times. Firm fruits cook for about 7 minutes, and soft fruits, about 3. Serve warm with ice cream.

COOKIES

Don't pass by those rolls of cookie dough in the dairy section! It's a real treat to have hot cookies on a camping trip, and if you don't want to start from scratch, these are a good substitute. If you don't have a cookie sheet that will fit into your grill, try double disposable trays or quadruple foil. Bake according to package directions, or over medium heat, top closed, 12 to 15 minutes.

INDEX

Almonds, 116
  Extract, 116
Anchovy paste, 111
Angel food cake, 115-119
Apples, 42, 76, 103, 108, 128
Apricots
  Dried, 116
  Jam, 116
  Nectar, 42
Asparagus, 85, 101
Avocados, 44

Bacon, 74, 83, 85, 98
Bananas, 42, 118, 126, 127
Barbecue, 31, 32, 41
Basil, 105
Beans, 35, 40, 68, 76, 79, 84, 85
Beef, 26, 71, 77
  Steak, 17, 20, 21, 29, 50, 51
  Ground, 29, 35, 73, 74, 77
Beets, 104
Bell peppers, 44, 57, 68, 70, 80,
  101, 102, 105
Biryani paste, 21, 91
Biscuits, 95
Blueberries, 42
Brandy extract, 116
Broccoli, 85, 87, 101, 104, 113
Buckwheat pancake mix, 127
Broth, 40, 69, 89, 91
  Beef, 75
  Chicken, 37, 38, 41
  Vegetable, 41
Buttermilk, 89, 90, 95, 98, 111
  Pancake mix, 127
  Powdered, 95

Cabbage, 37, 103
Candy, 121-123
  6-Minute Fudge, 121
  Chocolate Fudge, 122
  Rocky Road Fudge, 122
  Peanut Butter Fudge, 122
  Coconut Fudge, 122
  Coffee Fudge, 122
  Mocha Fudge, 122
  Key Lime Fudge, 123
Caraway seeds, 75
Carrots, 40, 42, 72, 73, 74, 85,
  101, 103
Celery, 40, 70, 74, 105, 106

Cayenne pepper, 19, 21, 33, 70,
  77, 86
Chard, 87
Cheese
  Blue, 108
  Cottage, 80
  Cheddar, 39, 41, 73, 79, 84, 90,
    93, 96
  Jack, 79
  Mozzarella, 67, 80
  Parmesan, 67, 68, 69, 80, 90,
    111
  Ricotta, 80
Cherries, 42
Chick peas, 104, 105
Chicken, 20, 25, 26, 30,
  41, 60, 64, 69, 70, 71, 72, 109
  Broth, 37, 38, 41
Chili, 76, 79
  Paste, 17, 91
  Powder, 17, 20, 21, 29, 32
Chiles, 76, 78, 79, 98
  Chipotle, 26, 31, 35, 41, 77, 91
  Green, 98
  Jalapeño, 39, 44, 79, 84, 96, 98
  Red, 29
Chocolate
  Bars, 120
  Chips, 122, 124
  Fudge sauce, 117
Chutney, 33
  About, 16
Cilantro, 35, 39, 44, 77, 82, 105,
  112
Clams, 39
Coconut, 118, 122, 126
Coffee, 122
Collard greens, 87
Cookies, 129
Coriander, 77
Corn, 35, 38, 44, 87, 88, 97, 98,
  105
Cornmeal, 98
Couscous, 72
Cranberries, 42, 63
Cream, 67, 75, 89, 126
Cumin, 17, 19, 20, 31, 39, 77, 84,
  90
Cucumbers, 43, 44, 104, 105
Curry, 19, 29, 72

SANTA FE, NEW MEXICO

Left New York, NY for points unknown.
50,000 miles later our home base is in
the Land of Enchantment instead of
mid-town Manhattan. How's that for a
change? Marilyn's told that story in
**FIRST WE QUIT OUR JOBS: How One
Work-Driven Couple Got on the Road to
A New Life.** And we still have thousands
of miles to go. You can meet us along the
way at www.recreationalpress.com. See
you out there!

Sandy and Marilyn